des
5/3/08

Grids

Grids: Creative Solutions for Graphic Designers

RotoVision

A RotoVision Book

Published and distributed by RotoVision SA
Route Suisse 9
CH-1295 Mies
Switzerland

RotoVision SA
Sales and Editorial Office
Sheridan House, 114 Western Road
Hove BN3 1DD, UK

Tel: +44 (0)1273 72 72 68
Fax: +44 (0)1273 72 72 69
www.rotovision.com

10 9 8 7 6 5 4 3 2 1

ISBN: 978-2-88893-001-3

Design: Studio Ink
Photography for Introduction: Andrew Penketh
Grid tutorials: Tony Seddon

Reprographics in Singapore by ProVision Pte.
Tel: +65 6334 7720
Fax: +65 6334 7721

Printed in China by Midas Printing International Ltd.

The CD and tutorials

The grids featured in this book are included on the accompanying CD, and have been recreated in both InDesign and QuarkXPress. To locate the grid you wish to utilize in either of these applications, simply look for the file name that matches the page number on which the grid appears in the book.

In addition to this useful resource, a series of tutorials that introduce readers to the process of grid design have been created exclusively for this book, and are available to download using the following URL.

www.rotovision.com/gridstutorials

Measurements

All measurements have been given in millimeters or points. If you prefer working in inches, most applications provide this option in the measurements palette.

Contents

Introduction

This whole business of grids is so difficult for graphic designers. Most of us love them. But we're scared of revealing any nerdy or, worse still, despotic tendencies so we jump nervously from foot to foot, simultaneously belittling and venerating the grid. We've got to appear to be casual about it—but not so much so that our peers think we're grid lightweights.

The problem is partly one of association. A grid is generally a series of straight vertical and horizontal lines so, if you're interested in grids are you "straight" in other ways too? This book sets out to demonstrate that, ultimately, it's not the notion of the grid that is important—it's the hand that constructs, the brain that computes, and the perspicacious eye that exploits these invisible structures.

A graphic-design grid is a bit like magic (now you see it, now you don't) sets of intersecting lines that help the designer decide where to put things, but that generally no one else sees. The benefits of using a grid are multifarious, ranging from the psychological to the functional, and, of course, the aesthetic. The grid embodies all the contradictions that designers struggle with. This is the designer's very own enigma code that can elevate design discourse to that of a science, and eradicate the creative block by "virtually" filling the blank page.

What is a grid?

A grid subdivides a page vertically and horizontally into margins, columns, inter-column spaces, lines of type, and spaces between blocks of type and images. These subdivisions form the basis of a modular and systematic approach to the layout, particularly for multipage documents, making the design process quicker, and ensuring visual consistency between related pages.

At its most basic, the sizes of a grid's component parts are determined by ease of reading and handling. From the sizes of type to the overall page or sheet size, decision-making is derived from physiology and the psychology of perception as much as by aesthetics. Type sizes are generally determined by hierarchy—captions smaller than body text and so on—column widths by optimum word counts of eight to ten words to the line, and overall layout by the need to group related items. This all sounds rather formulaic, and easy. But designers

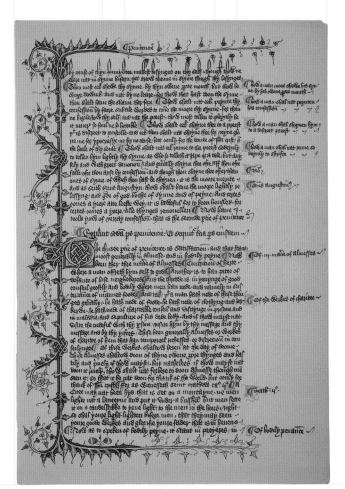

Left

This facsimile page is from a fourteenth-century English manuscript. The overall layout is asymmetric, and therefore surprisingly modern. The main column is positioned to the left of the page, with a large right-hand margin used for notes. All text is calligraphic and ranged left.

whose grids produce dynamic or very subtle results take these rules as a starting point only, developing flexible structures in which their sensibility can flourish.

The first five hundred years

Philosophers and linguists have argued that nothing exists in our consciousness unless it is named and we have a language with which to discuss it. Neither "graphic design" nor "grids" were talked about until the mid-twentieth century. Once named, complex grid structures comprising multiple columns, fields, baseline grids, and so on poured forth as never before, but it's not true to say that designers or their predecessors—commercial artists, printers, and scribes—hadn't been thinking about content, proportion, space, and form before this.

Even prior to typesetting and printing there were texts available to read. These were religious texts laid out by scribes in calligraphy. The pages were surprisingly modern, often using more than one column, with lettering that was ranged left, and color and variations in letter size used for emphasis. Just as the first cars resembled a horse-drawn carriage, the first printed pages took their cue from the manuscript page. But over time one major difference was introduced—justified setting. In this, spaces between words in continuous text are adjusted in each line so that columns align on both left and right sides. Although manuscript pages were symmetrical when viewed as spreads, the ranged-left lettering made them essentially asymmetric. With justified setting came 450 years of symmetry, and it wasn't until the twentieth century that this convention was truly challenged.

Left

Although derived from calligraphic forms, this lettering is actually type. Taken from a late-sixteenth-century English Bible, this page shows how printers quickly adopted symmetry. The text is justified and the two columns placed symmetrically on the page, with hanging notes also positioned according to a central axis.

Proportion and geometry

From the beginnings of printing (from the mid-fifteenth century) until the Industrial Revolution (late eighteenth century), the book was the primary output of printing. Apart from verse, type was generally set in one justified column per page, placed symmetrically on the spread with larger outer margins than inner, and a larger margin at the foot than at the head. But just as each decision made in minimal art is hugely significant, so too were the relative relationships of these few elements on the page. The proportions of these pages and margins were determined by geometry, concerned with the relation of points, lines, surfaces, and solids to one another rather than their measurement.

There are many geometrical constructions that can produce a beautiful page, but the golden section is usually cited as the most successful. As it is a geometrically derived form, it can be drawn with a setsquare and a compass—no measuring required. For those who do like to know measurements, the relationship of short to long side of a golden rectangle is 1:1.618. Many contemporary designers find this apparently irregular ratio unsettlingly chaotic, but others feel that the number sequence at its core has almost magical properties. By adding the lengths of the long and short edges it is possible to arrive at the next measurement in the sequence to give a bigger rectangle of the same proportions. This also works in reverse in order to make a smaller rectangle.

Adding two numbers to find the next in a series is also the basis of the number progression of the Fibonacci sequence, named after the thirteenth-century Italian mathematician who first identified it in many natural forms, from the arrangements of petals to the spirals of seashells. A combination of the golden section and Fibonacci sequence (1, 1, 2, 3, 5, 8, 13, etc) was often used to determine the overall proportion of the page and margins of the classical book.

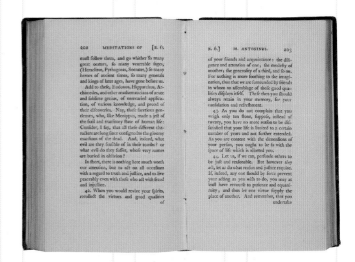

Above
This spread from The Meditations of Marcus Aurelius Antoninus, published in 1792, uses the golden section to determine the text area, and the Fibonacci sequence to arrive at relative margin sizes (inner margin 3 units; top and outer margins 5 units; bottom margin 8 units). The gutter is treated as the central axis, and there is one column of text. The outer and bottom margins are larger than the inner and top. These optical adjustments ensure that the text doesn't appear to be falling off the bottom of the page.

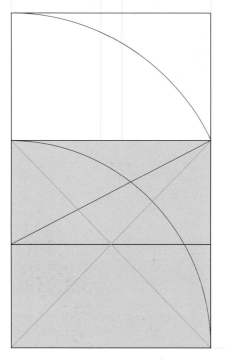

Left
This diagram shows how to draw a golden-section rectangle using only a set square and a compass. The resulting proportions are considered to be some of the most aesthetically pleasing. Start by using a set square to draw a right angle. Place a compass in one corner and draw an arc to arrive at a square, then draw a line horizontally through its center. Use the compass to join the two points shown to complete the rectangle.

The next hundred years

The Industrial Revolution marked the beginning of a capital-based economy, with mass production at its heart. Graphic design was born, although still not named as such. Its job was to communicate diverse messages to an increasingly literate people. The rise in print output was phenomenal—posters, leaflets, and advertising of all kinds, newspapers, timetables, and all manner of information-based design. Suddenly designs competed for attention. Images, initially in the form of engravings and then as photographs, had to be incorporated along with an ever-expanding array of display typefaces. Highly skilled and educated printers stayed firmly in the land of the book, while jobbing printers and compositors struggled to lay out this diverse material for which the classical book was not a useful precedent.

Toward the end of the nineteenth century, artists and thinkers identified this as a problem that had to be solved. Although the work produced by William Morris and the Arts and Crafts movement may appear very different from that of modernism, Arts and Crafts was its forerunner in one important respect. Morris believed that form and function were inextricably entwined. Running almost concurrently with these ideas were the revolutionary cubist experiments of Picasso and Braque,

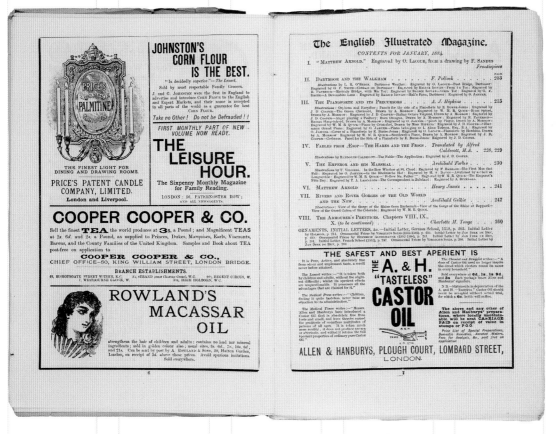

Left

Design as we know it was born partly in response to the Industrial Revolution. As this spread from the English Illustrated Magazine of 1884 shows, designs were suddenly competing for attention. The resulting visual confusion may have a certain charm, but these random layouts were confusing and often inaccessible. Contemporary designers considered this a problem to solve and started to explore different theoretical approaches to their work.

who were exploring how to represent 3-D forms on 2-D planes, producing increasingly abstract results. Artists, and then designers, were influenced by this work, and re-evaluated composition as a result.

The early twentieth-century art movements—futurism, dadaism, surrealism, constructivism, suprematism, and expressionism—also had an influence on the development of the grid. Artists were united in trying to represent a new, industrialised age exemplified by speed of travel and faster communication. They recognized the power of the word and broke with all previous print tradition by using type at conflicting angles or on curves; introducing extreme variation in type sizes; using drawn, abstracted letterforms; and generally ignoring the vertical and horizontal nature of type. For the first time, space was used as a dynamic component in typographic layout. The ethos that underpins this work was the antithesis of the rational and logical approach implicit in the grid. But in drawing such a resolute line under the past, it opened the door to de Stijl, the Bauhaus, and typographers like Herbert Bayer and Jan Tschichold, who called for some order to be imposed on what seemed like fractured chaos.

de Stijl, the Bauhaus, and Jan Tschichold

In 1917 Dutch architect, designer, and painter Theo van Doesburg founded de Stijl. The importance of this movement to the grid is that it explored form as determined by function, and placed this in a political context. Arguing that simplicity of form was accessible and democratic, its members advocated minimalism, using only rectilinear forms, and eradicating surface decoration other than as a byproduct of a limited color palette: the primaries plus black and white. The typographers affiliated to de Stijl wanted to apply these ideas in the real world, not just for their artistic cause. Designers like Piet Zwart and Paul Schuitema used these principles to produce commercial advertising and publicity materials.

The Bauhaus opened its doors in Weimar, Germany, in 1919, with the architect Walter Gropius as its Director. His belief that architecture, graphic art, industrial design, painting, sculpture, and so on were all interrelated had a profound impact on the development of typography and graphic design long after the school was forced to close by the Nazis in the 1930s. Within an astonishingly short period of time, graphic artists were marrying analytical skills with abstract form to arrive at mass-produced designs determined as much by political idealism as by a desire for self-expression. In 1925, Herbert Bayer was appointed to run the new printing and advertising work-shop. He paid attention to typographic detail, experimenting with a limited typo-graphic palette in order to achieve greater visual clarity and easily navigable pages.

During the late 1920s and the 1930s, typographer Jan Tschichold set out his typographic principles in two seminal books: *The New Typography* (1928), and *Asymmetric Typography* (1935). Tschichold's work was more refined than much of that which had preceded it. He wrote of typographic consistency as a necessary precursor to understanding, described designers as akin to engineers, and argued compellingly for asymmetry as a central tenet of modernism. It was the logical way to lay out text that is read from left to right, and produced "natural" rather than "formalist" solutions to the new design challenges than classicism, with its enforced central axis. In his work Tschichold explored subtle horizontal and vertical alignments, and used a limited range of fonts, type sizes, and type weights.

Josef Albers: Wall picture, etched in black-and-white double-layer glass. 1928.

Subjectless painting is usually called abstract, but to be precise what it deals with is not abstract, but real – a line, a circle, an area signify them-selves, while in representative painting they stand for something else. Therefore it is not wrong to apply the word 'abstract' to representative painting. The expression 'absolute painting' is also objectionable. Theo von Doesburg and the AC group were right when they first used the term 'concrete painting' in 1930. This term however, is not suitable in the English language.

A painting with a subject consists of two things and most people think only of one, namely the subject. They are pleased if a picture re-

80

Project for a poster by Jan Tschichold, 1932 (not printed). An exercise in balance. Such a design might still be used to advertise electronic music.

Left

This spread and throw-out is from Jan Tschichold's seminal work Asymmetric Typography, *originally published in 1935. In it Tschichold argued that typographic consistency is a necessary precursor to understanding, and described designers as akin to engineers. His work was nevertheless aesthetically refined and dynamic. Here he explains the parallels between abstract art and typographic layout.*

The grid and Swiss typography

Early modernists had explored layout, space, and scale. They had talked of the democratizing benefits of mass production, and had used the language of science as much as art. They had argued for consistency and minimalism as a mark of design confidence and greater accessibility. During WWII, and in the decades that followed, these ideas coalesced into a coherent design manifesto with a new design device at its core—the grid.

The grid and Swiss typography are synonymous. Switzerland was neutral during the war. Not only did it attract many intellectual refugees, including designers like Jan Tschichold, but also most

peacetime activities continued as normal, and supplies of such things as ink and paper weren't rationed. Added to this, publications had to be set in its three official languages—French, German, and Italian—which called for a modular approach, using multiple column structures.

Several Swiss artist/designers, most notably Max Bill and Richard Paul Lohse, explored systematic forms in their paintings concurrently with graphic design, while the graphic designers Emil Ruder and Josef Müller-Brockmann both wrote educative texts explaining what grids were and how to use them. They approached the subject with great rigor, arguing passionately that "integral design" required structures that would unite all the elements in both 2-D and 3-D design: type, pictures, diagrams, and space itself. Despite their enthusiasm

for order and precision, they both understood the value of artistic intuition.

"No system of ratios, however ingenious, can relieve the typographer of deciding how one value should be related to another... He must spare no effort to tutor his feeling for proportion... He must know intuitively when the tension between several things is so great that harmony is endangered. But he must also know how to avoid relationships lacking in tension since these lead to monotony." **Emil Ruder**, *Typography*

The grid and the design philosophy of which it is a part have been criticized for placing the narcissistic designer at the heart of the solution, and generating formulaic solutions that are mechanistic, unyielding, and rigid. But for Ruder, Müller-Brockmann, and many other designers since, the grid was the natural response to a design problem. It was also a metaphor for the human condition, and was found in all areas of human endeavor.

"Just as in nature, systems of order govern the growth and structure of animate and inanimate matter, so human activity itself has, since the earliest times, been distinguished by the quest for order... The desire to bring order to the bewildering confusion of appearances reflects a deep human need." **Josef Müller-Brockmann**, *Grid Systems in Graphic Design*

Right

The ingenuity of the "A" paper sizing system appeals to designers who are interested in modular approaches to design. For the true modernist, working with standard paper sizing is more economic and celebrates mass production. But, for designers who want to usurp the system, there are countless ways to subdivide the sheet sizes to arrive at more unusual formats.

Left

Several post-War Swiss designers are the best-known exponents of the grid. This spread is from Josef Müller-Brockmann's Grid Systems in Graphic Design, *in which he explains, in meticulous detail, how multicolumn and field-based grids can be used flexibly to achieve any number of different layouts, in both 2-D and 3-D work.*

Below

This spread and throw-out from Anthony Froshaug's Typographic Norms, *published in 1964, explores the modular measurement systems that were at the heart of typography and letterpress printing at the time, and which are the basis of many grid structures today.*

Grids and mathematics

The difference between grids as we know them and the page layouts of the past rests in increased flexibility and mathematical dexterity. This starts with considering format and ends with baseline grids, for which lines are often subdivided into units as small as 2pt. The computer has made greater precision easy, and contemporary grids subdivide the page into small component parts that can be combined in numerous ways that still ensure cohesion in the design. Small columns are joined to make wider columns, numbers of baseline units are joined to make fields, and so on.

Karl Gerstner's grid for the journal *Capital*, designed in 1962, is still often cited as near-perfect in terms of its mathematical ingenuity. The smallest unit in Gerstner's grid, or matrix as he called it, is 10pt—the baseline to baseline measurement of the text. The main area for text and images is a square, with an area above for titles and running heads. The cleverness lies in the subdivision of the square into 58 equal units in both directions. If all intercolumn spaces are two units, then a two-, three-, four-, five-, or six-column structure is possible without any leftover units.

The grid made visible

Grids are generally made visible only through use, but some designers have exposed the workings of the graphic design machine to demonstrate that the grid is something not only of utility, but also of beauty. Once visible, the precision of the grid acts as evidence of design credibility, and its purity of form has a mystical draw.

The Dutch designer Wim Crouwel pioneered the application of systematic design in the Netherlands during the 1950s and 1960s. His identity for the Vormgevers exhibition at the Stedelijk Museum in Amsterdam in 1968 used an exposed grid in the layout of posters and catalogs, which was also the basis of the lettering. In 1990, issue 7 of 8vo's influential journal *Octavo* ran grids with coordinates, like maps, under

Above

The Swiss designer Karl Gerstner's 1962 grid for the periodical Capital *is near perfect. His unit, both horizontally and vertically, was 10pt—the baseline to baseline measurement of the text type. The type area was a square of 58 units. Allowing for intercolumn spaces, this gave Gerstner grids of two, three, four, five, and six columns and fields.*

Right

Dutch designer Wim Crouwel is known for his exploration and experimentation with grids. In this poster for the Vormgevers exhibition in 1968, he made the grid visible. This device then formed the basis not only for the layout, but also for the lettering.

each spread. *Octavo* called their method of working "visual engineering."

"To get things built, you have to be able to describe them... The act of specifying requires one to define the structure of a design very precisely... It places one's design under intense scrutiny in terms of structure and logical process. Very different to the 'drag and drop' computer screen environment, where close enough is often good enough." **Mark Holt and Hamish Muir**, *8vo: On the Outside*

Designer Astrid Stavro has taken this one stage further. Inspired by a diverse set of grids, from the Gutenberg Bible to the *Guardian* newspaper, Stavro's GRID-IT notepads celebrate the usually invisible graphic-design grid in its purist form—unused and unsullied. Perhaps we can take this as a sign that designers no longer worry about being a little nerdy or despotic.

Left

Having started the journal Octavo, designers 8vo edited and designed it from the mid 1980s to the early 1990s. The design often explored systematic and modular approaches, but in issue 7 the designers chose to reveal their methods by giving the grid coordinates, like a map, and printing it as a background to each page.

Above

Italian designer Astrid Stavro worked on the Grid-it! Notepads project while studying at London's Royal College of Art. The intention is to celebrate the notion of the grid in its pure form. Each pad shows a different grid. These range from Tschichold and Müller-Brockmann classics to the Gutenberg Bible and Guardian newspaper. [Photographer: Mauricio Salinas]

Catalogs, leaflets & brochures

Below The voice of the
Society—our magazine,
The Designer issues 21 to 24

it will be firmly established within the design sector, increasing in regularity.

The Designer Now at issue number 24 the magazine has moved on from being the voice of the Society to having also developed a following in its own right. The most recent issue shows a confidence in tackling design sector issues that impact upon business and the community in discussing the demise of one of the UK's leading automotive manufacturers with a history of design innovation.

Over the past 2 years—contrary to the norm—the costs for the magazine have been reduced by good management and generous sponsorship. It was never the intention that the magazine should be dependent on advertising revenue but recently this has increased as the title becomes more prominent. More importantly are the partnerships and affinity marketing opportunities being exploited by the magazine. These are seeing members benefit from special offers on books, events and subscriptions and the Society as a whole benefiting from favourable costs on many of its activities. The title is now becoming a valuable asset and will be protected over the coming years. Contrary to original thoughts of outsourcing the magazine to a contract publisher, the Society will continue to produce the *The Designer* in-house and exploit it to further CSD strategy and initiatives.

Design Sector Relationships For many years the Society was forced to withdraw from joint initiatives in the design sector due to lack of funds. It was often the case that the Society generously funded projects that some members deemed questionable and of little real value to the membership. Our current financial strength, imaginative and relevant initiatives in education and practice and potential sector

influence sees CSD once again as a focus of attention. Over the past few years the Society has focussed its attention on servicing its members and developing a strategy for long term growth and influence in a global design economy. In order to follow through this strategy we will remain selective as to the relationships, collaborations and projects we enter into.

The focus for the next 2 years will be relationships with education as part of our overall recruitment policy of younger members. However, we will maintain the qualities the Society is well known for, those of promoting professional practice and quality in design education.

The Society is currently developing bespoke courses/workshops for graduate members in collaboration with The Cultural Industries Development Agency (CIDA). These will be aimed at those starting out in their chosen career and instilling best practice at the earliest possible stage.

Now in its 5th year, *Free Range* is a programme set up to support and promote new creatives. This major annual event showcases the work of art & design courses from all over the country bringing the very best of the nation's graduates together in a festival of exhibitions.

Graduate work, from across the disciplines, is exhibited by the numerous colleges involved, from art and design to photography and interiors. In addition to the event, the work of thousands of exhibitors is showcased in the official *Free Range* catalogue and website.

Next year's event will see the first collaboration with CSD and this will provide an ideal opportunity to recruit Graduate members, promote course accreditation and enhance further CSD's educational profile.

The development of the Design Association will also allow us to build strong relationships with a diverse range

Council Members
As at 31/12/04

Summary Statement of Financial Activities

Balance Sheet

CSD ANNUAL REVIEW 2004

Design: Brad Yendle at Design Typography

Design Typography found inspiration for this 24-page annual review in Karel Marten's SUNschrift book covers from the 1970s and 1980s. Marten's covers are printed in two colors, creating a third color through overprinting. They say that necessity is the mother of invention—designer Brad Yendle introduced this technique here not only to make visible the structure of the page, but also to enliven some of the inconsistent and undistinguished photography that had been supplied. Yendle describes his grid as fairly standard—four columns with a deeper-than-average top margin—but by introducing the offset colored blocks, he has simultaneously broken the grid and reinforced the clarity of his design.

GRID SPECIFICATIONS

Page size (trimmed)	150 x 297mm
Top margin	7mm
Bottom margin	15mm
Outside margin	7mm
Inside margin	7mm
Number of columns	4
Gutter width	4mm
Extras	Baseline grid, 12pt starting at 87.2mm

ISLINGTON

Islington has long been known as one of London's most fashionable and stylish boroughs. It draws its vibrant character from around the world and there is a real sense of community in this thriving and prosperous area. Home to some of the most diverse shopping in London, it offers unrivalled choice.

Crafted by CARROT.

L'ÉCOLE
L'ÉCOLE

L'ÉCOLE

Available January 2007

CARROT

L'ÉCOLE

L'École, a former Victorian schoolhouse and architectural landmark, located on the northern fringes of Islington, has been crafted into 52 spacious apartments by Carrot. L'École consists of two buildings, a sympathetic conversion of the Victorian schoolhouse and a contemporary new building. The two buildings sit side by side, designed in unison and working together to create a distinctive development where 21st-century technology is mixed with classic Victorian elegance. The development embodies Carrot's philosophy of creating individually crafted spaces with a modern style, whilst retaining a warm, sensuous feel.

ISLINGTON

Islington has long been known as one of London's most fashionable and stylish boroughs. It draws its vibrant character from around the world and there is a real sense of community in this thriving and prosperous area. Home to some of the most diverse shopping in London, it offers unrivalled choice.

Crafted by CARROT

GRID SPECIFICATIONS

Page size (trimmed)	330 x 310mm
Top margin	25mm
Bottom margin	18mm
Outside margin	25mm
Inside margin	15mm
Number of columns	8
Gutter width	5mm
Extras	Baseline grid, 21.5pt starting at 35.7mm

L'ÉCOLE PROPERTY BROCHURE

Design: Brad Yendle at Design Typography

L'École, a former school in north London, was redeveloped by Carrot into a variety of apartments. The building took shape in several phases, so designers Brad Yendle and Zoë Bather were briefed to develop a flexible system that could be updated and added to easily over time. This requirement informed all aspects of the design. The publication is loose-leaf and loop bound. The binding is not only practical, but also unusually utilitarian in feel—both Design Typography and its client were keen to ensure that the publication reflected the detailing of the development and wasn't dismissed as a predictably glossy promotion. The grid is based on eight small columns that can be used in different combinations to accommodate text, images, maps, plans, and diagrams.

Contemporary architecture and spacious layouts
dominate the feel of the new build apartments at
L'École. Building in a U-shape around the communal
courtyard garden has given the development a real
sense of community.

The Winter Gardens add a unique focal feature to
the front elevation, providing a fabulous enclosed glass
space all year round, offering seclusion and serenity in
this bustling London borough.

At the top of the buildings sit the stunning
penthouses, whose abundant use of glass ensures they
are always flooded with light. The penthouse lifestyle
offered at L'École is one of true indulgence – whilst
relaxing on the terrace, one can enjoy panoramic views
across Islington.

Crafted by CARROT

KITCHENS
Individual Swedish-designed black high-gloss 'Kvanum'
kitchens combined with white 'Corian' worktops
Fully integrated 'Siemens' appliances, dishwasher,
fridge freezer, ceramic hob, oven & extractor hood

BATHROOMS
Underfloor electric heating
'Porcelanosa' porcelain floor & wall tiles in 'Cube Nature'

BEDROOMS
Bespoke floor to ceiling wardrobes in master bedrooms
Satellite TV point
Telephone socket
Wall lights
Carpets

GENERAL
Oak wide-board floors
Fully wired for home entertainment system installation

SPECIFICATION

Throughout L'École, detail and finish are second to
none and this is synonymous with the Carrot brand and
concept. Each L'École apartment is individually crafted
by Carrot with precise attention to detail using high-
quality materials to the highest level of specification.

Crafted by CARROT

Q – WHERE IS L'ÉCOLE SITUATED?   **A – JUST 2 STOPS AWAY FROM PARIS ON THE EUROSTAR**

ALL THAT YOU WILL EVER NEED ...

Whether it is a theatre, university, museum, green space, a place to buy a good transport links that you need, living at L'École will ensure that it is right on your doorstep.

1 King's Cross, St Pancras, Eurostar
2 Arsenal, Highbury Fields, Metropolitan University
3 Upper Street, N1 Shopping Centre, Business Design Centre, Antiques Theatre, Antiques Arcade
4 Sadler's Wells Theatre, Exmouth Market, Clerkenwell
5 The City, St Paul's
6 Camden Passage Market
7 Hampstead Heath
8 Tate Modern, London Eye
9 Regent's Park
10 2012 Olympic Site

Details: L'ÉCOLE

Details: CARROT

CARROT ©

Carrot Limited is a niche property developer specialising in bespoke residential and mixed use schemes in city centres – creating inspiring urban homes which focus on space and design quality.

Carrot was formed in 2001 by Tim Corr. Tim has been in the Central London property business since 1975, by way of estate agencies and consultancy, with a particular dexterity in acting for developers and house builders in acquisitions, site disposal and marketing.

Prior to setting up Carrot, Tim co-founded CYZ. For the past 12 years his management of CYZ has ensured that it has built a reputation as a 'class act' in urban regeneration and warehouse conversions, notably in Clerkenwell, London.

Tim founded Urban Construction Management Ltd (UCM) in 2001, the construction company for all Carrot projects. This relationship ensures a tighter control of the cost and management of the construction process, allowing Carrot to exercise hands-on control of its schemes. Since formation, UCM have consistently delivered projects to budget and to planned timescales.

Central London is Carrot's core market. However Bristol in the South West, where Carrot is already developing, has been identified as having similar regeneration potential and market characteristics, allowing the Company's expertise to be fruitfully applied in a new city.

For more information about L'École and other developments, please contact Charlotte Steedman.

Carrot Ltd
48 Britton Street
London EC1M 5UL
T +44 (0)20 7251 3999
F +44 (0)20 7251 8008
E charlottesteedman@carrotltd.com
www.lecolecarrot.com

Grids: Creative Solutions for Graphic Designers

LOST SOULS LOOKBOOK

Design: Julian Harriman-Dickinson at Harriman Steel

The humble postcard was the inspiration behind this promotional "lookbook" for Lost Souls clothing company, designed by Julian Harriman-Dickinson. Consisting of four postcards inserted into the folds of a double-sided A3 (297 × 420mm [11¾ × 16½in]) poster, the overall design utilizes the grid generated by the folding process. Graphic-design grids are generally invisible to the end user and, although determined by format, are additions to it. Here the grid is completely visible and inseparable from the format. This reinterpretation of the grid is, by its nature, three-dimensional, and creates unexpected relationships between text and image as the structure unfolds and the content is revealed.

GRID SPECIFICATIONS

Page size (trimmed)	167 x 193mm
Top margin	7mm
Bottom margin	7mm
Outside margin	9mm
Inside margin	12mm
Number of columns	5
Gutter width	4mm
Extras	6 horizontal fields

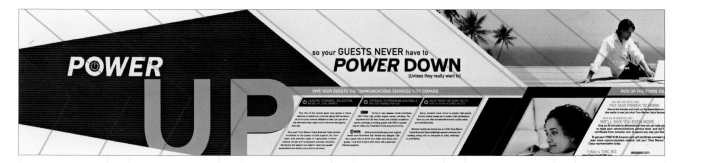

TIME WARNER CABLE SAN DIEGO MAILER

Design: Saima Malik at Origin Design

Origin was briefed to design direct mail that would capture the dynamism of southern California and help revitalize Time Warner's business-to-business brand image in the region. To accentuate the forward-looking ambition of his client, designer Jim Mousner used a slanting grid, and introduced angled columns along with images cropped to fit oblique abstract forms. Cleverly, the rotated grid is mirrored horizontally across the top and bottom of the page so that arrow-like shapes are created where columns and shapes meet. The dynamic is further emphasized through the use of angled die-cuts, bold typography, and double-hit fluorescent colors.

GRID SPECIFICATIONS

Page size (trimmed)	784.225 x 171.45mm
Top margin	7.938mm
Bottom margin	7.938mm
Outside margin	7.938mm
Inside margin	7.938mm
Number of columns	4, interior at 141.5° rotation
Gutter width	1.588mm
Extras	2 horizontal fields

ANNUAL REPORT 2003

Content

Publisher:
CROATIA osiguranje d.d.
Head office
Zagreb, Trg bana J. Jelačića 11
Prepared by:
Accounting and analysis department
Corporate licence department
Sales and marketing department
Design: Boris Ljubičić, STUDIO INTERNATIONAL Zagreb
Printed: Kratis d.o.o., Zagreb

Basic Information on Croatia Insurance Company

Croatia Insurance Company was founded on 4th June 1884 under the name of the Croatian Insurance Association. It was founded upon adoption of the Basic rules of the Zagreb Joint-Insurance Association. At the time of political domination of politicians disinclined to Croatia, which was under the rule of Austro-Hungarian Monarchy, the foundation of Croatia Insurance Association was motivated by the desire to prevent the capital outflow, therefore, promoting Croatian national interests. Its primary task was to engage in insurance popularization and self-protection against fire risks through the fire safety means and measures.

Shareholder structure on December 31st, 2003

The total number of shareholders on 31.12.2003 was 3.052.
There are all common shareholders with the Croatia Insurance, and 2.25% are preferred shareholders. The largest portion shareholder is the Croatian Privatization Fund that is in possession of the 257.042 shares of Croatia Insurance Company (27%, 71% of which are common shares and 3% preferred shares), or 21.2% of the shareholder structure, on 31.12. 2003.

STATEMENT OF CHANGES IN CAPITAL AND RESERVES

DESCRIPTION	Equity capital Kuna	Security reserves Kuna	Other reserves Kuna	Profit in the current year Kuna	TOTAL Kuna
Status on December 31, 2002	452.867.202	162.132.452	8.592.402	43.254.231	677.267.283
Profit distribution for the year 2002					
Security reserves	0	22.133.991	0	-22.133.991	
Stockholders' dividend	0	0	0	-43.125.260	-43.125.260
Profit in the current year	0	0	0	74.530.656	74.530.656
Status on December 31, 2003	452.867.202	185.166.443	8.592.402	74.530.656	711.274.941
Note	3.6.c.	3.6.c.	3.6.c.		

The notes on pages 9 to 59 are integrative part of the present financial reports.
Certified auditor's report - page 1

a) Transferable premium, net from re-insurance
The transferable premium value, net from reinsurance was balanced by the authorized actuary of the Company. It is shown as follows:

DESCRIPTION	31.12.2002. Non-life insurance Kuna	% share	Increase / Decrease in % 03/02.	31.12.2003. Non-life insurance Kuna	% share
A) Gross transferable premium					
Transferable premium - functional part	637.142.339	81.621	11.351	709.436.383	83.621
Transferable premium - overheads	148.243.141	18.681	11.671	164.827.488	15.431
Total gross transferable premium	785.485.480	100.001	11.351	874.259.791	105.001
B) Re-insurance portion					
Re-insur. portion in the transfer. premium-functional part	0	0.001	-	-24.427.528	-2.651
Re-insur. portion in the transfer. premium-overheads	0	0.001	-	-1.353.147	-0.141
Total re-insurance portion	0	0.001	-	-23.880.667	-3.051
Total A+B	781.485.480	100.001	0.001	866.379.382	105.001

b) Mathematic reserve for life insurance, net from re-insurance
Mathematic life insurance reserve, net from re-insurance, was also was balanced by the authorized actuary of the Company. It is shown as follows:

DESCRIPTION	31.12.2002. Non-life insurance Kuna	% share	Increase / Decrease in % 03/02.	31.12.2003. Non-life insurance Kuna	% share
Mathematic reserve - gross	620.216.796	100.001	25.371	777.687.917	100.001
Re-insurance portion in the mathematic reserve	-4.033	0.001	-5.141	-3.843	0.001
Total	620.216.763	100.001	25.371	777.383.929	100.001

Mathematic life insurance reserve is shown in accordance with the positive legal provisions and accounting standards further described in the note 3.18 (a) of the present Report.

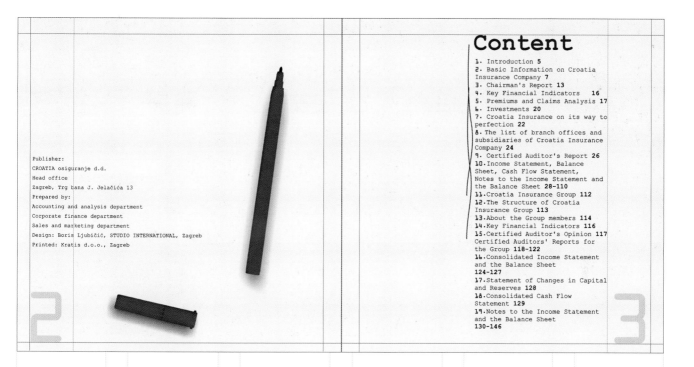

Publisher:
CROATIA osiguranje d.d.
Head office
Zagreb, Trg bana J. Jelačića 13
Prepared by:
Accounting and analysis department
Corporate finance department
Sales and marketing department
Design: Boris Ljubičić, STUDIO INTERNATIONAL, Zagreb
Printed: Kratis d.o.o., Zagreb

Content

GRID SPECIFICATIONS

Page size (trimmed)	210 x 210mm
Top margin	10.3mm
Bottom margin	5.3mm
Outside margin	8mm
Inside margin	11.5mm
Number of columns	2
Gutter width	N/A
Extras	N/A

CROATIA ANNUAL REPORT 2003

Design: Boris Ljubicic at Studio International

Croatia Osiguranje is one of Croatia's most reputable insurance companies. Although it is keen to build on its reputation and long history, the company is aware that its successes have to be presented accessibly. Its annual report is full of complex tabular matter along with facts and figures. Designer Boris Ljubicic's aim was to ensure easy navigation and facilitate understanding of this dense document through simple graphic means. The grid introduces plenty of white space and enables a clear and clean layout of information, text, tables, and charts. The colored-pencil device is a playful and humanizing element used to make hierarchy clear through underlining and highlighting details of the content.

U.S. GREEN BUILDING COUNCIL

ANNUAL REPORT

Grids: Creative Solutions for Graphic Designers

GRID SPECIFICATIONS

Page size (trimmed)	200.025 x 254mm
Top margin	2.54mm
Bottom margin	22.225mm
Outside margin	6.35mm
Inside margin	6.35mm
Number of columns	3
Gutter width	N/A
Extras	N/A

**U.S. GREEN BUILDING COUNCIL
ANNUAL REPORT**

Design: Richard Chartier

Richard Chartier wanted the U.S. Green Building Council (USGBC) annual report to be architectural in feel, so decided to use the grid as a metaphor for construction. His solution was to "build" the design so that it gradually reveals its own supporting architecture—a grid of vertical columns and horizontal fields. This idea is developed throughout the publication and its various supplements, including a financial insert in which the baseline grid is exposed. Chartier also introduced a variety of illustrative elements, juxtaposing them with his clean, abstract grid to emphasize the relationship between man-made and natural structures.

Exhibitions

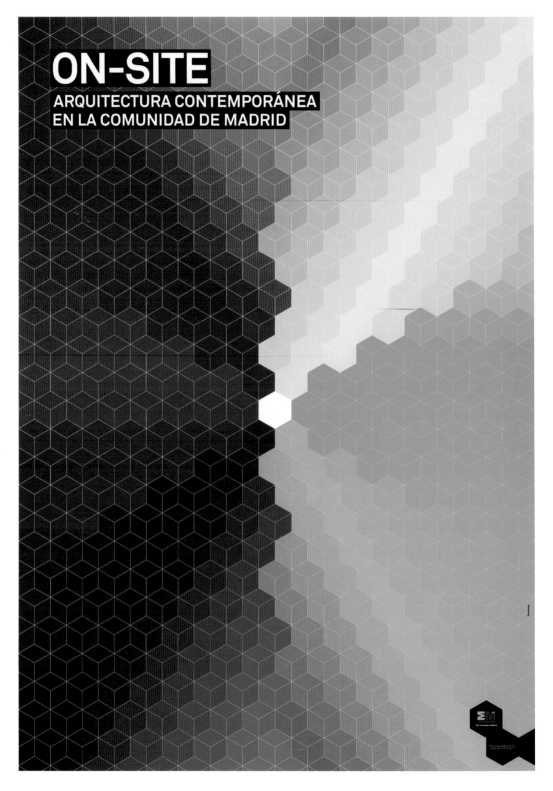

ON-SITE
ARQUITECTURA CONTEMPORÁNEA
EN LA COMUNIDAD DE MADRID

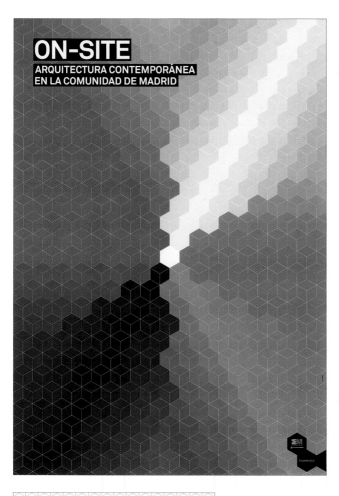

GRID SPECIFICATIONS

Page size (trimmed)	Resizable, as required
Top margin	½ base unit
Bottom margin	½ base unit
Outside margin	½ base unit
Inside margin	½ base unit
Number of columns	Flexible
Gutter width	2.5mm
Extras	Grid developed from base unit—hexagon

ON-SITE EXHIBITION GUIDELINES
Design: BaseDESIGN

The exhibition On-Site: New Architecture in Spain documented recent Spanish architectural innovation. A Museum of Modern Art initiative, the exhibition opened in New York before moving to Madrid. BaseDESIGN's graphic solution uses the architectonic form of a cube (suggested by the perspective of the hexagon) as a basis for the identity. The three visible sides of the cube symbolize the exhibition, tours, and talks, which are also color-coded as red, blue, and green, respectively. Although not a conventional typographic grid, this is a highly flexible modular system that provides the framework for a range of color and pattern combinations to communicate the diversity in form, scale, and geography of the exhibits.

ON-SITE
ARQUITECTURA CONTEMPORÁNEA EN LA COMUNIDAD DE MADRID

Es una plataforma desde la que mirar la arquitectura contemporánea a través de tres acciones simultáneas: ON-SITE EXPO, exposición de proyectos, ON-SITE TOUR, itinerarios temáticos y ON-SITE TALK ciclo de conferencias.
ON-SITE profundiza en la arquitectura de la Comunidad de Madrid destacando sus edificios y proyectos relevantes y dando voz a arquitectos que hayan desarrollado su actividad en la región.

Abierto todos los días
Septiembre - octubre de 10:00 a 20:00 h.
Noviembre - diciembre de 10:00 a 19:00 h.
Enero de 10:00 a 18:00 h.

ON-SITE
EXPO
ARQUITECTURA EN ESPAÑA, HOY
22.09.06 - 14.01.07
PABELLÓN VILLANUEVA
REAL JARDÍN BOTÁNICO DE MADRID

La exposición, elaborada por el MoMA y organizada por PromoMadrid, presenta los desarrollos arquitectónicos más significativos realizados en España del 2000 al 2005. En ella se muestra la extraordinaria diversidad del panorama actual español, que destaca internacionalmente por su capacidad de englobar diferentes tendencias arquitectónicas, arquitectos de distintas nacionalidades y generaciones, en toda la geografía nacional.

ON-SITE
TOUR
ITINERARIOS DE ARQUITECTURA EN LA COMUNIDAD DE MADRID
REAL JARDÍN BOTÁNICO
CALLE ESPALTER, 9
SALIDA AUTOBÚS 19:00 h.
HASTA EL 12 DE NOVIEMBRE

Recorridos por edificios significativos a través de ciclos temáticos con los que redescubrir la arquitectura de la Comunidad de Madrid.

Martes: TOUR-A. Grandes Maestros: Sota, Oíza
Miércoles: TOUR-B. Grandes Maestros: Fisac, Torroja
Jueves: TOUR-C. Desde Arriba
Viernes: TOUR-D. Casa a Casa
Sábado: TOUR-E. Orgánicos y Ye-yé
Domingo: TOUR-F. Ciudad Museo

Tours para grupos y visitas concertadas, de martes a domingo a las 12:00 h.
Imprescindible reservar
(info@rms.com /91 524 02 19)

ON-SITE
TALK
CONFERENCIAS SOBRE ARQUITECTURA ACTUAL
AUDITORIO DE PROMOMADRID
SUERO DE QUIÑONES, 34

Dos ciclos de coloquios que proponen un acercamiento a la arquitectura contemporánea con una mirada particular a la Comunidad de Madrid; un encuentro entre estudios participantes en la exposición y otras figuras relevantes del mundo de la arquitectura.

Para actualizaciones de este programa consultar la web
www.promomadrid.com

TALK ON-SITE
Algunos de los estudios de arquitectura presentes en la exposición expondrán su trabajo en coloquio. La propuesta de diálogo permitirá profundizar sobre diversos aspectos de los trabajos presentados desde nuevos puntos de vista.

2 octubre
Iñaki Ábalos (Ábalos&Herreros). 18:00 h.
Dominique Perrault. 19:30 h.

23 octubre
Jacob Van Rijks (MVRDV). 18:00 h.
Tuñón&Mansilla. 19:00 h.

CONTEXTO MADRID ON-SITE
Una reflexión sobre aspectos concretos de la arquitectura en la Comunidad de Madrid.
Arquitectos nacidos, establecidos o que hayan trabajado en la Comunidad de Madrid describirán su contexto a través de la mirada a un edificio, a un artista o a un arquitecto.

24 octubre
Alberto Campo Baeza. 18:00 h.
William J.R.Curtis. 19:30 h.

8 noviembre
Aranguren&Gallegos. 18:00 h.
Sancho&Madridejos. 19:30 h.

14 noviembre
Alejandro Zaera (F.O.A.). 18:00 h.
Federico Soriano. 19:30 h.

+INFO
WWW.MADRID.ORG
WWW.PROMOMADRID.COM

WIM CROUWEL EXHIBITION CATALOG
Design: SEA

SEA self-published this catalog to accompany an exhibition of
Wim Crouwel posters held at its gallery in London. Renowned for
his fascination with grid structures and a systematic approach to
design, Crouwel's posters juxtapose highly structured letterforms,
often hand-drawn, with carefully composed typographic layouts.
SEA's catalog uses a nine-column grid divided horizontally into
11 fields. This structure gives great flexibility while ensuring
unity throughout the publication. Columns are joined in different
combinations to allow for varying text measures. Both images and
text hang at different heights determined by the fields. By leaving
columns and fields empty, SEA has used space creatively to add
emphasis and to help the reader navigate the page.

Fernand Léger

Silkscreen, 88x60cm
Stedelijk Van
Abbemuseum
Eindhoven
1957

stedelijk
van abbemuseum
eindhoven

fernand léger

dagelijks geopend
van 10-17 uur
zondag
van 13-17 uur
dinsdag- en
donderdagavond
van 20-22 uur

2 februari tot
10 maart 1957

Mason Wells
North Design

06 — 07   I was disappointed that I had to comment on the Léger poster, not because I dislike it, but because
I wanted to pay homage to Vormgevers (a personal favourite, and I hazard a guess, the one everyone else
wanted to pass comment on). But examining an early piece such as this allows one to re-assess things
in terms of the evolution of Crouwel's work.
    It goes without saying that Crouwel's posters meet all the right criteria in terms of what constitutes
a good poster — they are legible, they work at varying proximities, they are compositionally perfect and they
are built on content. You almost take it for granted that all the right bits are in the right places.
    What really makes his work so outstanding, is the custom letterforms and typefaces (which feature
in seven of the eight posters on display). In the case of the Léger poster, the title is created as an interlocking
linear structure, presumably in reference to the cubist forms of the artist. This would be easy on a Mac, but
three decades before, it brought along a new set of problems.
    Crouwel placed no boundaries on himself and his constant re-invention of typeforms (whether
manipulated or drawn from scratch) kept his work free from the dogmas associated with the work of many
of his contemporaries, ensuring that each new artwork was fresh. Looking at this poster, it's easy to see how
it pre-empts his later work such as Vormgevers, Visuele communicatie and New Alphabet.
    What is hard to comment on are the bits that contextualise it. Tangible elements such as colour,
print process and scale — even mistakes such as misaligned registration and over-specified colour trap —
become impossible to pass comment on when all one has as reference are miniscule reproductions (in this
case an absolutely knackered Mode en Module and a few Dutch design books). It's like criticising a piece
of architecture without visiting the building — you have to go there and experience it to truly understand it.

Fernand Léger

Silkscreen, 88x80cm
Stedelijk Van
Abbemuseum
Eindhoven
1957

stedelijk
van abbemuseum
eindhoven

fernand léger

dagelijks geopend
van 10-17 uur
zondag
van 13-17 uur
dinsdag- en
donderdagavond
van 20-22 uur

2 februari tot
10 maart 1957

Mason Wells
North Design

06 — 07
    I was disappointed that I had to comment on the Léger poster, not because I dislike it, but because I wanted to pay homage to Vormgevers (a personal favourite, and I hazard a guess, the one everyone else wanted to pass comment on). But examining an early piece such as this one allows one to re-assess things in terms of the evolution of Crouwel's work.

    It goes without saying that Crouwel's posters meet all the right criteria in terms of what constitutes a good poster — they are legible, they work at varying proximities, they are compositionally perfect and they are built on content. You almost take it for granted that all the right bits are in the right places.

    What really makes his work so outstanding, is the custom letterforms and typefaces (which feature in seven of the eight posters on display). In the case of the Léger poster, the title is created as an interlocking linear structure, presumably in reference to the cubist forms of the artist. This would be easy on a Mac, but three decades before, it brought along a new set of problems.

    Crouwel placed no boundaries on himself and his constant re-invention of typeforms (whether manipulated or drawn from scratch) kept his work free from the dogmas associated with the work of many of his contemporaries, ensuring that each new artwork was fresh. Looking at this poster, it's easy to see how it pre-empts his later work such as Vormgevers, Visuele communicatie and New Alphabet.

    What is hard to comment on are the bits that contextualise it. Tangible elements such as colour, print process and scale — even mistakes such as misaligned registration and over-specified colour trap — become impossible to pass comment on when all one has as reference are miniscule reproductions (in this case an absolutely knackered Mode en Module and a few Dutch design books). It's like criticising a piece of architecture without visiting the building — you have to go there and experience it to truly understand it.

GRID SPECIFICATIONS

Page size (trimmed)	210 x 265mm
Top margin	5mm
Bottom margin	5mm
Outside margin	10mm
Inside margin	10mm
Number of columns	9
Gutter width	2.5mm
Extras	11 horizontal fields

Vormgevers
(Designers)

Offset, 95x64cm
Stedelijk Museum,
Amsterdam
1968

Mark Holt
Mark Holt Design

14—15 For this poster, Crouwel revealed the grid he had used on all his previous posters (and the later posters he would produce) for the Stedelijk Museum. Place a number of Stedelijk posters alongside Vormgevers and it is remarkable to see the grid used time and time again to anchor each poster's design elements.

Each grid square and corresponding interval is equal to five units, which predetermines the height of the two sizes of font used on Vormgevers. The diameter of the rounded corners of the larger font, is equal to the width of a single unit. The font's form grows out of the grid itself, letter and grid are one. Resolved it certainly is. And if anyone needed proof that black and white need not be a poverty then surely this poster is it.

My favourite detail? The numeral five which starts the second text line, set to the x-height of the font and placed directly under the 's' of Stedelijk. In this context, quite possibly the most bizarre five I think I've ever seen.

22 — 23

| Fernand Léger 1957 | Hiroshima 1957 | Beelden in Het Heden 1959 | Edgar Fernhout 1963 | Vormgevers 1968 | Visuele Communicatie Nederland 1968 | Het Nederlandse Affice 1890 — 1968 1968 | Lucht/Kunst 1971 |

One of Crouwel's best known posters, and a personal favourite of his. Drawn without the aid of graph paper, the poster's strong diagonal black lines reveal Crouwel's initial point of reference — it was a continuation from his New Acquisitions poster of 1956.

The Léger poster is simply constructed, with a letter 'r' which is formed from part of a pure circle, rather than being optically corrected.

Crouwel was very impressed by Léger's paintings and he has described this piece as being a typographic, if somewhat poetic, interpretation of the artist's work.

Designed in the same year as the Léger poster, this poster marked an exhibition of Japanese drawings based on Hiroshima. The background colour was similar to that of Japanese lacquer and the word Hiroshima is based on a small Grotesk — the way the letters were constructed determined their very tight spacing.

Crouwel wanted the word Hiroshima to appear heavy and threatening, and likens the ascenders and serifs extended to singed chimneys rising up from the black form.

A poster which was designed for an exhibition of sculpture. Crouwel designed the poster in portrait format to look like a landscape with three vertical sculptures, but it was always hung horizontally by mistake.

The bands of colour represent earth, sky and the horizon and the letterforms form the three sculptures. The letters are tightly spaced and the serifs extended to give the effect of a solid sculpture — they were individually drawn, pushed together and then painstakingly drawn again.

In this poster for an exhibition of paintings by Edgar Fernhout, Crouwel was influenced by the artist's abstract landscapes, which were painted using small brush-strokes. The letterforms which were influenced to some extent by Tschichold, were divided into four equal parts, two above and two below the 'horizon' that Crouwel created through the middle of the text, also in reference to the artist's work.

Crouwel only designed these letters at the time of making the poster — he did not make them into a complete alphabet until four years later.

One of Crouwel's most talked about pieces, this poster featured a visible grid that was used for the layouts of all of the catalogues Crouwel designed for the Stedelijk.

The original graph sheets were printed in light grey — for this poster, Crouwel made the lines more visible and composed the letterforms inside them. The letterforms were a precursor to Crouwel's Fodor typeface, which was designed three years later.

Designed for the Dutch Art Directors Club, this poster combines simplified pointed letterforms, all three points wide, which sit on a background inspired by the first bar codes.

The letterforms were reduced to very simple forms and are similar to those in Crouwel's soft alphabet, designed for his Claes Oldenburg poster of 1970.

Although it is a poster about visual communication, Crouwel admits that it is the most illegible poster that he has made.

This poster was created for an exhibition about posters and features a folded down corner in the top left hand side, which reveals the Stedelijk marque and is a reference to the transient nature of the artform.

The letterforms are constructed around a square, and give rise to a strong sense of perspective, creating striking diagonals. The letters that form the word 'Affiche' go off the page on both sides, suggesting a fleeting glimpse of a poster as you walk past it.

This poster is for an exhibition that was devoted to art made with air — pieces that were inflatable. Crouwel rounded off the letterforms (which are constructed from a narrow Grotesk) and pushed them together to give them a feeling of being blown full of air.

Both the outline and the spaces between the letters become very significant and the speech bubble is another (somewhat more literal) take on the subject matter.

HORROR VACUI

C ities in the Netherlands, from Groningen in the north to Maastricht in the south, are undergoing a remarkable transformation. While Dutch cities, with the exception of Almere, are scarcely growing at all in terms of population, a great deal of building is going on in road-straddling construction in the pipeline; dual land use is an undeniable trend, manifested in road-straddling construction and tunnelling beneath or building on top of existing buildings. Open areas, derelict zones, and disused port and industrial areas are, or soon will be, turned into new fragments of city, with urban densities

and urban-looking buildings; consolidation is under way in city centres and around the railway stations; in nearly every city residential and office tower. The gaps in the urban fabric that were an accepted part of Dutch cities until the mid 1980s, are fast disappearing

Urban implosions in the Netherlands

Text: Hans Ibelings
Photos: Roel Backaert

A s cidades holandesas, desde Groningen no norte até Maastricht no sul, estão a sofrer um processo de transformação interessante. Embora as cidades sejam construídas com excepção de Almere, as cidades holandesas não cresçam em termos de número de habitantes, o número de construção de andares extra sobre edifícios já existentes.

e tipo de construção urbano; nos centros das cidades e junto das grandes estações ferroviárias constrói-se em grande escala, em praticamente todas as cidades são construídos grandes arranha-céus para habitação ou escritórios; a duplicação da superfície tornou-se em termos de número de habitantes, o número de vagos e espaços derrubados tem vindo a agigantar uma tendência incontornável. Espaços e áreas desocupadas e enormes áreas de portos e indústria não utilizadas são transformadas, com uma densidade

Texto Hans
Fotog
Roel

01 Almere, Stadshart
02 Amsterdam, Arena precinct
03/04 Amsterdam, Zuidelijke IJ-oevers
05/06 Amsterdam, Westelijke Tuinsteden
07 Amsterdam, Zuidas
08 Arnhem, Station precinct
09/10 The Hague, Beatrixkwartier/De Resident
11 Eindhoven, Smalle Haven
12 Enschede, Van Heekplein
13 Groningen, Ciboga
14 Lelystad, Stadshart
15 Maastricht, Céramique
16 Rotterdam, Müllerpier
17 Rotterdam, Wijnhaven
18 Rotterdam, Zuidelijke Maasoever
19 Tilburg
20 Utrecht, Leidsche Rijn
21 Utrecht, De Uithof
22 Zaanstad

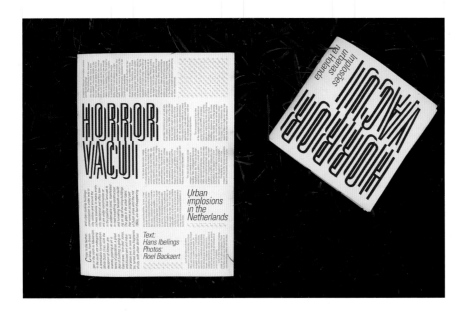

Grids: Creative Solutions for Graphic Designers

GRID SPECIFICATIONS

Page size (trimmed)	Panels: 1100 x 1100mm/
	Booklet: 170 x 235mm
Top margin	Panels: 52.5mm/Booklet: 7.8mm
Bottom margin	Panels: 200mm/Booklet: 7.8mm
Outside margin	Panels: 52.5mm/Booklet: 7.8mm
Inside margin	Panels: 52.5mm/Booklet: 0mm (interior)
Number of columns	Panels: 5/Booklet: 5 (sideways)
Gutter width	Panels: 30mm/Booklet: 5mm
Extras	N/A

HORROR VACUI EXHIBITION PANELS

Design: Arjan Groot and Julia Müller

These panels and booklet were designed for the traveling exhibition Horror Vacui: Urban Implosions in the Netherlands, initially shown at the Lisbon Architecture Triennial. The exhibition looked at how gaps are filled within the urban fabric of Dutch cities—the term "horror vacui" translates as "fear of empty spaces." The designers took this theme as the starting point for their design. They filled any empty spaces on their pages with a graphic pattern influenced by textile weavings and Scottish tartans. Reminiscent of op art, this pattern creates a kind of visual vertigo appropriate to the overall subject matter. These repetitive graphic marks are, in themselves, an elaborate grid, and form the basis of the more conventional typographic grid used for the text and image layouts.

HORROR VACUI

Urban implosions in the Netherlands

Cities in the Netherlands, from Groningen in the north to Maastricht in the south, are undergoing a remarkable transformation. While Dutch cities, with the exception of Almere, are scarcely growing at all in terms of population, a great deal of building is going on. Open areas, 'overshot' zones, and disused port and industrial areas are, or soon will be, turned into new fragments of city, with urban densities and urban-looking buildings; consolidation is under way in city centres and around the railway stations; in nearly every city residential and office towers are under construction or in the pipeline; dual land use is an undeniable trend, manifested in road-straddling construction and tunneling beneath or building on top of existing buildings. The gaps in the urban fabric that were an accepted part of Dutch cities until the mid 1980s, are fast disappearing.

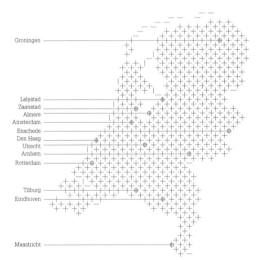

Groningen

Lelystad
Zaanstad
Almere
Amsterdam
Enschede
Den Haag
Utrecht
Arnhem
Rotterdam

Tilburg
Eindhoven

Maastricht

This exhibition is produced by the Netherlands Architecture Institute in collaboration with A10 new European architecture, with financial support from the Netherlands Architecture Fund.

Curators: Hans Ibelings + Kirsten Hannema. Exhibition design: Marta Malé-Alemany + José Pedro Sousa (ReD). Graphic design: Arjan Groot + Julia Müller. Photography: Roel Backaert. Production: Suzanne Kole + Marinke van der Horst. Supervisor: Martien de Vletter. International coordinator: Agnes Wijers

Special thanks to: AAS Architecten, ARCADIS Bouw en Vastgoed BV, Architectenbureau Art Zaaijer, Architectenbureau Marlies Rohmer, Architectuurstudio Herman Hertzberger, Atelier Rijksbouwmeester, Benthem Crouwel Architekten BV, Bouwfonds MAB Development, Bureau B+B stedebouw en landschapsarchitectuur, City of Eindhoven, City of Tilburg, Claus en Kaan Architecten, De Architekten Cie, De Zwarte Hond, Department of Physical Planing and Economic Affairs Groningen, Department of Physical Planning Amsterdam, Dick van Gameren architecten B.V., Dienst Stedelijke Ontwikkeling – City of The Hague, dS+V Rotterdam, (EEA) Erick van Egeraat associated architects, FARO Architecten bv, FPW Rotterdam, hvdn Architecten, JHK Architecten, Jo Coenen & Co Architecten, KCAP Architects&Planners, Köther | Salman | Koedijk | Architecten bv, Meyer en Van Schooten Architecten BV,

MVRDV, NL Architects, OD 205 architectuur bv, Office for Metropolitan Architecture, OMS Beheer bv (City of Lelystad and William Properties bv), ONL [Oosterhuis_Lénárd], Ontwikkelingsbedrijf Rotterdam, Pierre Gautier architecture, PPKS Architects Ltd., Project Organisation Stationsgebied – City of Utrecht, Projectbureau Amsterdam Zuidas – City of Amsterdam, Projectbureau Zuidelijke IJ-oevers – City of Amsterdam, Rijnboutt Van der Vossen Rijnboutt bv, S333 architects, Soeters Van Eldonk Architecten, Stadsdeel Geuzenveld-Slotermeer – City of Amsterdam, Tania Concko Architectes, THALEN/BASELINE, UN Studio, Van Sambeek & Van Veen Architecten, Vera Yanovshtchinsky architecten, vof ontwikkelingscombinatie IMA (ING, MOESbouw, AM), West 8 urban design & landscape architecture b.v., Wiel Arets Architects, Ymere Ontwikkeling, Zwarts & Jansma Architects

Groningen   Ciboga

Rotterdam   Wijnhaven

considerada então como «demasiado *engagé*». Tendo por objectivo único transformar-se num agrupamento «completamente atrasado mental», logo ficou decidido que os Ena Pã deveriam assumir como seu objectivo fazer a «pior música possível», utilizando apenas um ou dois acordes, a qual seria ainda servida por letras «absolutamente idiotas». Procurariam a todo o custo transformar-se num grupo de rock português que, «tal como os Sex Pistols ou os Ramones», exibisse a sua «mediocridade de modo transbordante e esplendoroso». A ideia fez o seu caminho, que deve já ficar aqui enunciado. Na futura formação musical, espécie de braço musical da homeostética, esteve, além de Vieira, Francisco Ferro. O primeiro concerto, ou melhor, a primeira «representação de concerto rock», aconteceria ainda em Dezembro de 1982 – no meio de uma festa operária e num prédio em construção, a ela tendo apenas assistido Portugal, Proença, uma rapariga anónima e seu cão – e o disco inicial viria a ser publicado cinco anos depois: trata-se de um single em vinil com duas músicas apenas,

«Pão, Amor e Totobola» e «Telephone call». A partir de 1984, muitas das canções dos Ena Pã 2000 passaram a ser escritas por Fernando Brito, ao lado de Manuel Vieira. Em Anelhe, os passeios pelo campo e as imensas refeições, naquele Verão de 1982, foram intercalados também com a realização de várias pinturas. Pedro Portugal, que desde aí se atribuiu no movimento o papel do sujeito que cola as partes e as faz operar – «os budistas chamam a estas pessoas pontes», assinala a propósito –, começou a registar fotograficamente todas estas viagens, bem como as performances efectuadas pelos seis artistas e companheiros na ESBAL, daí resultando um acervo composto por milhares de negativos de «fotos oficiais» ou «autorizadas». E é facto indesmentível que a memória homeostética adquire, através das fotografias de Pedro Portugal, uma extensão

desconhecida de outros agrupamentos estéticos. Os três passaram ainda pelo festival de Vilar de Mouros, onde viriam a conhecer as irmãs Medeiros, Maria e Inês, que pouco depois começariam a aparecer no Grupo de Teatro da Escola de Belas-Artes, animado por Xana e que viria também a ser integrado por Vieira e Proença. Estes dois partiriam, ainda em meados de Agosto, para o Algarve e em Lagos – onde se encontrava Xana de férias – tocaram bandolim e guitarra nas ruas durante dias seguidos, tendo com isso conseguido arrecadar algumas moedas. Rumaram em seguida à Fuzeta, localidade em que lhes surgiria a personagem Capitão Nemo, cujas cartas, relatando viagens imaginárias, foram escritas num espírito de absoluta desconversa. No mês seguinte, Vieira e Portugal foram até Paris tirar mais fotografias e ver o que «estava a acontecer».

Grids: Creative Solutions for Graphic Designers

GRID SPECIFICATIONS

Page size (trimmed)	252 x 356mm
Top margin	15mm
Bottom margin	15mm
Outside margin	25mm
Inside margin	15mm
Number of columns	12
Gutter width	4mm
Extras	Baseline grid, 14pt

6 = 0 EXHIBITION CATALOG

Design: Lizá Ramalho, Artur Rebelo, and Nuno Bastos at R2 design

This catalog accompanied an exhibition by 1980s Portuguese art collective Homeosteticos, held at the Serralves Museum of Contemporary Art, Porto. The title, 6=0, reflected how under-appreciated this group of six artists felt. Designers Lizá Ramalho, Artur Rebelo, and Nuno Bastos emphasized this notion by reversing the equation of the title and placing a zero on the front cover and a six on the back.

Poemas Homeostéticos

Edição
ASA DE ICARVS

Grids: Creative Solutions for Graphic Designers

The selection of work for the publication was made in collaboration with contributing artist Pedro Portugal by putting work up on the studio walls and editing intuitively. The composition of the pages attempts to capture this; the scattering of images within the multi-column grid reflects the organic nature of the selection process, and resembles the composition in progress on the studio wall. The grid is designed to allow flexibility, but still gives the publication a strong overall structure.

URBAN VOIDS EXHIBITION CATALOG

Design: Lizá Ramalho, Artur Rebelo, and Liliana Pinto at R2 design

This promotional material for the Lisbon Architecture Triennial was designed to reflect the overarching theme of the event—urban voids. Designers Lizá Ramalho, Artur Rebelo, and Liliana Pinto wanted to use graphic forms to communicate ideas of abandonment, and also to draw attention to city spaces that are often overlooked. By choosing a stencil font, and showing it in its fragmented form, the designers produced what at first appears to be a dislocated composition. But, by printing on different densities of translucent paper (as used in architectural projects), the name of the event becomes clear once the publication is folded to size. The overall grid structure is simple, but the hanging heights of the text further reinforce the sense of isolation and temporary dislocation.

Grids: Creative Solutions for Graphic Designers

GRID SPECIFICATIONS

Page size (trimmed)	420 x 594mm
Top margin	10mm
Bottom margin	10mm
Outside margin	10mm
Inside margin	10mm
Number of columns	4
Gutter width	5mm
Extras	Baseline grid, 11pt

vazios urbanos
urban voids

Trienal de Arquitectura de Lisboa / Lisbon Architecture Triennale 2007

Trienal de
Arquitectura
de Lisboa 2007
Lisbon Architecture
Triennale 2007

31/05 — 31/07

Principais exposições / Main exhibitions

DENTRO DO PAVILHÃO / IN THE PAVILION

www.trienaldelisboa.com

vazios urbanos
urban voids

Trienal de Arquitectura de Lisboa / Lisbon Architecture Triennale 2007

Trienal de
Arquitectura
de Lisboa 2007
Lisbon Architecture
Triennale 2007

31/05 — 31/07

Principais exposições / Main exhibitions

DENTRO DO PAVILHÃO / IN THE PAVILION

www.trienaldelisboa.com

KRAH: FIRST CONGRESS OF CROATIAN ARCHITECTS POSTER

Design: Boris Ljubicic at Studio International

These posters were commissioned by the Croatian Architects Association to raise the profile of architecture within politics. They set out 10 objectives and argue for policies to benefit the built environment. Designer Boris Ljubicic decided to use 3-D numbers as a starting point for his posters. He started with a traditional column-and-field grid, and used this to organize the composition of the objects. The camera angle and dramatic lighting create strong diagonals that animate the overall design. These posters work in tandem; the Ten Proposals poster uses the body of the numerals as the basis for the text while Building at the Coast, which addresses the context in which these tenets might be applied, utilizes the space around the figures.

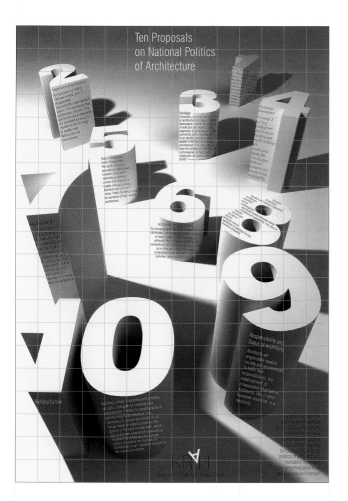

GRID SPECIFICATIONS

Page size (trimmed)	595 x 840mm
Top margin	To bleed
Bottom margin	To bleed
Outside margin	To bleed
Inside margin	To bleed
Number of columns	14
Gutter width	N/A
Extras	Base unit, 42mm square

Illustrated books

The Art of the Jester

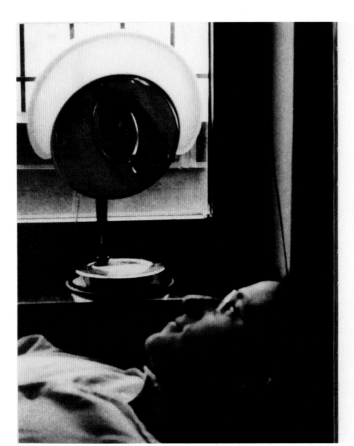

Chip Kidd. Photograph by Duane Michals, 2001.

Pull a book at random from your bookcase and look at its cover. That is all you need to do to travel back to that specific moment in your life when you first read it. As compact as a time capsule, a book jacket holds forever the memory of the brief cultural period when it was in print. But a short shelf life is the price a book jacket must pay for leaving a vivid impression in the mind. My 1987 hardcover edition of Tom Wolfe's *The Bonfire of The Vanities*, so promising when it came out during the heady days of the Reagan administration, looks and feels today like a dear old friend wearing a toupee.[1] However, the fact that most book jackets look dated within a couple of years of their publication does not take anything away from their graphic appeal. One of the things we love about books is the way they age along with us.

Yet today, newness is considered a critical design element of a book jacket. Indeed, when I survey bookstores, the future obsolescence of the latest best-sellers' covers is the furthest thing from my mind. Even though I am aware that the current jackets will one day have the same emotional patina as award-winning jackets designed or art directed a decade ago by Louise Fili, Carin Goldberg, Sara Eisenman, Paula Scher, Frank Metz, Krystyna Skalski, Fred Marcellino or Neil Stuart, I cannot help but be seduced by the allure of instant modernity that the new books seem to capture. One of the things that tells me that a book is brand new is the presence of photography on its cover. Over the last couple of years, I have been conditioned to equate the use of conceptual photography on American book jackets with cutting-edge, contemporary literature. In contrast, if a book has an illustrated jacket, I regret to admit that I assume that its content is somewhat behind the curve. Graphic profiling, like racial profiling, is an inescapable reality in the world in which we live today.

The now popular photographic approach was originally pioneered in the late 1980s by a group of young designers working for the Knopf Publishing Group. Famous for its emblematic Borzoi logo, the Knopf

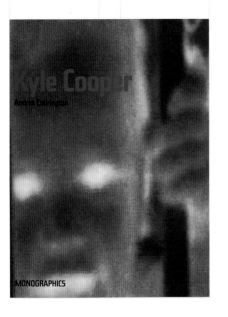

Donnie Brasco

Director - Mike Newell, 1997
Titles - Kyle Cooper (dir.)
for Imaginary Forces

One of the first main titles to be done under the Imaginary Forces name, Donnie Brasco is an introduction to a moody and evocative that is had our fine letter- first peering it above the film itself. Using a combination of predominantly black and white and colour stills shot at surveillance-style - complete with Kodak markings and grainy print scribblings - Cooper photographs an unsettling sequence about friendship betrayal and the implications of relationships gone sought in the underworld. Accompanied by a delicate piece of music by Patrick Doyle, the grainy still images become animated thanks to a carefully choreographed edit that becomes a slow fade then teased by rapid cut action sequences and the occasional piece of live footage. The titles begin and end with a scene of Johnny Depp's look-singed eyes looking from outside - an expansive city in the midst of New York noir guns.

DONNIE BRASCO

GRID SPECIFICATIONS

Page size (trimmed)	189 x 238mm
Top margin	5mm
Bottom margin	10mm
Outside margin	8mm
Inside margin	18mm
Number of columns	6
Gutter width	5mm
Extras	Baseline grid, 13.25pt starting at 45.5mm

MONOGRAPHICS SERIES

Design: Brad Yendle at Design Typography

Each book in Laurence King's Monographics series concentrates on the work of one creative practitioner. The series style has to be recognizable, but flexible, and has to act as a fairly neutral backdrop to the work featured. These considerations informed designer Brad Yendle's decision to create what he describes as a considered, but quite austere design. Herbert Spencer's *Typographica* magazine and the *Graphis* annuals from the 1960s were his inspiration. Yendle's grid is a multicolumn structure that can accommodate continuous text, captions, and index easily. Its large top margin introduces welcome breathing space to pages that include visual examples and formats from a range of disciplines—movie stills and titles, book covers and spreads, prints and comic books.

Véronique Vienne

Chip Kidd

Laurence King Publishing

Kyle Cooper. Photograph by Michael Grecco.

Through the Glass Darkly

Kyle Cooper is a postmodern paradox. He is an iconoclast who loves what he transgresses, whether the tenets of modernist typography, the idea of apple-pie America or even the belief in an all-loving, all-powerful God. He is by nature betwixt and between, not quite fitting into the commercial world of Hollywood and not entirely at home in the realm of high-design discourse. He is a true-believing Christian whose oeuvre has often lingered on the sinister themes of murder and madness. The work that he has created over the past decade – first at R/Greenberg and then at Imaginary Forces, the studio he cofounded in 1996 with Peter Frankfurt and Chip Houghton – distinctively plays off this tension to great effect.

In an age predicated on irony – the knowing collusion between auteur and audience via winking references made at breakneck speed – Cooper's work comes into bold relief, for it is marked by something that seems all but lost in our cleverness-as-king culture: earnestness. This may sound an odd description for a designer who first came to fame with the opening titles for David Fincher's 1995 film Seven, a sequence characterized by degraded, hand-scrawled type and nerve-jangling imagery. But Cooper has realized something important: desecration is all the more effective when the ideals being torn down are ones that are dearly held by the desecrater.

Kyle Cooper's short-form artistry is particularly appreciated in a culture known for its collective attention deficit disorder because it delivers intense experiences in quick bursts. The fact that such jags of entertainment have snuck into the unassuming cultural spaces of legally mandated credit sequences is a testament to both the creative urge and, perhaps, consumer culture's discomfort in the presence of blank, unmediated space. Cooper himself displays a tendency toward fitful absorption – darting associatively in conversation from one topic to the next, multi-tasking to such an extent that many of the interviews that fill his dictionary-sized book of press clippings were given on his cell phone while driving the freeways of Los Angeles.

Grids: Creative Solutions for Graphic Designers

104

105

The Cold Six Thousand
James Ellroy
Main photograph – Mell Kilpatrick
2001 New York ALFRED A. KNOPF
[Hardback]

48

The blurred colour photograph of a neon
Las Vegas landscape sets the location for
a tale of violence and corruption amid the
desert casinos. The bloodied crime scene
offers a macabre invitation to enter a world
peopled with amoral characters who both
repel and fascinate.

White Jazz
James Ellroy
Photograph – Robert Morrow
1992 New York ALFRED A. KNOPF
[Hardback]

"Chip Kidd frames the front cover in
pristine white – a color at once stark,
innocent and inviting. Centered in that
white expanse: an LAPD patrol car door
shot full of holes. The potential book
buyer/reader has been presented with
a statement and a challenge – forceful,
simple, elegant: Read This Book!"
– James Ellroy

American Tabloid
James Ellroy
Main photograph – Mell Kilpatrick
2001 New York ALFRED A. KNOPF
[Paperback]

49

The saturated and grainy colour images
of eyes and lips highlight our voyeuristic
attraction to scenes of bloodshed and
mayhem. The vintage shot of a crime
scene makes reference to the American
underworld in the years before and after
the Bay of Pigs.

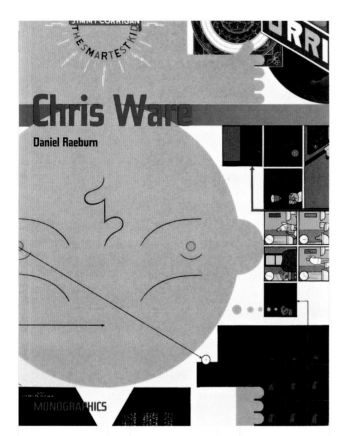

Chris Ware

Daniel Raeburn

MONOGRAPHICS

Daniel Raeburn

Chris Ware

Laurence King Publishing

6

A New Style:
American Design at Mid-Century 1950–1959

'Modern businessmen have come to recognize that design can and should be used to express the character and identity of business organizations. Design is a function of management, both within an industry and the world outside it. Industry is the institution that reaches further into our civilization than government and therefore has a greater opportunity and responsibility to influence the quality of life.'

Herbert Bayer quoted in *A Tribute to Herbert Bayer*, 1979

THE AMERICAN SCENE

The American economy continued to boom in the 1950s. Despite the police action in Korea, Americans generally knew peace, prosperity and conformity in this decade. The nation had a certain naïvety, a simple and optimistic approach to life which preceded the turbulent changes to come in the 1960s. It was the calm before the storm. Improved mass-market technology made television sets affordable for many more people and brought advertising for a vast range of products straight into people's homes. Strikingly different product forms became available. The critic Thomas Hine referred to the 1950s as a time when 'everything from a T-bird to a toaster took on a shape that seemed to lean forward, ready to surge ahead.' It was as if the streamlined Art Deco style of the 1930s had been updated for a new audience. Detroit produced cars with exaggerated tail fins and gleaming chrome.

But despite the bright and shining optimism, the early 1950s were also the era of the McCarthy Communist witch hunts, the beginning of a deep dissent in the land – a conflict between liberalism and xenophobic conservatism. Jack Kerouac's book *On The Road* (1957) and Allen Ginsberg's poetry gave voice to the underground counterculture of the Beat Generation. Music lost its squeaky-clean image and became dissonant and more subversive. Art became more expressive and abstract. The definition of art was even challenged by Claes Oldenburg's soft sculptures and Allan Kaprow's 'Happenings'. The art of New York finally eclipsed that of Paris – the Americans had arrived on the scene with a vengeance. The 1950s was the decade that saw the emergence of the painter Jackson Pollock. His work grew out of a dynamic, improvisational Zeitgeist that characterized both the progressive jazz of the time and the writings of the Beat Generation. Socially, the beginnings of the civil rights movement happened in 1950 as Rosa Parks sparked the bus boycott in Montgomery, Alabama. Signs of deep change were on the horizon as Americans basked in the postwar optimism while they cruised around the new suburbs in their gas-guzzling cars with huge fins on each rear fender.

Opposite top *Portfolio* magazine was a major professional achievement for Alexey Brodovitch. In this experimental arts publication he was able to combine optimum editorial and design quality. This two-page spread from 1951 presented an article on the painter Jackson Pollock. Scale contrast in the photography plus the understated typography combines to create a layout of great elegance.

Opposite bottom Advertising designer Robert Gage worked for Doyle Dane Bernbach Inc. He produced this ad for the New York rye bread company, Levy's. A whole series of similar ads followed, appearing even as late as 1967. These ads represented the simple, direct, humorous and sometimes controversial approach to print advertising that was common in the 1950s.

66

JACKSON POLLOCK

ADVERTISING IN THE 1950s

By the late 1940s and early 1950s, an increasing consciousness about graphic design and designers was evident because Modernism became more visible on the creative scene. Design became a more dominant force in the corporations and in the advertising business. An important debate occurred between typographic purists and those who believed in excitement and experimentation. The most effective examples of design in the 1950s were able to mediate these differences, excite their readers and be legible. In advertisements, copy was shorter, headlines more brief, and text functioned to support the illustration. Photography, both colour and black-and-white, was the dominant medium of advertising illustration. Creativity was the big word in this decade, especially in advertising. Towards the end of the 1950s, at a New York Art Directors Club conference, keynote speakers stated that designers were now moving away from being just layout men to assuming creative responsibility for the whole job. Many designers opened their own businesses; companies specializing just in graphic design. In corporations, the title 'graphic design' finally meant something. Those who practised this

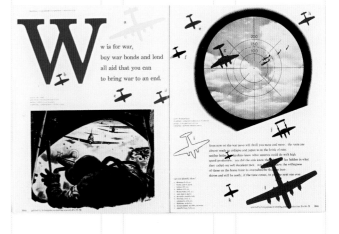

You don't have to be Jewish

to love Levy's
real Jewish Rye

A New Style: American Design at Mid-Century 1950–1959   67

Contents

1 The Basis for the New: The Cradle of Modernism 1850–1899 — 7

2 A New World Forming: The Impact of Modernism 1900–1919 — 15

3 American Design in Transition: Traditional to Modernism 1920–1929 — 33

4 Into the Design Scene: Modernism Arrives in America 1930–1939 — 47

5 At War and After: The Creative Forties 1940–1949 — 83

6 A New Style: American Design at Mid-Century 1950–1959 — 135

7 Design Since Mid-Century: Diversity and Contradiction 1960–1999 — 157

W is for war,
buy war bonds and lend
all aid that you can
to bring war to an end.

Grids: Creative Solutions for Graphic Designers

AMERICAN MODERNISM: GRAPHIC DESIGN 1920 TO 1960

Design: Brad Yendle at Design Typography

The design for this book needed to be anonymous and discrete. Many of the designers included now have iconic status—Lester Beall, Alexey Brodovitch, Lou Dorfsman, Paul Rand, Ladislav Sutnar, and Massimo Vignelli—and their work is often extremely bold and strong. The book explores the extraordinary influence that European émigrés had on American design. Appropriately, designer Brad Yendle used two complementary fonts, one designed by a German—Futura —and the other by an American—New Caledonia. Referring to Jost Hochuli's work as a book designer, Yendle developed a six-column grid. By combining these small columns in different configurations, the text, captions, and images are easily accommodated.

GRID SPECIFICATIONS

Page size (trimmed)	280 x 215mm
Top margin	23mm
Bottom margin	27.5mm
Outside margin	15mm
Inside margin	16mm
Number of columns	6
Gutter width	4mm
Extras	Baseline grid, 15.5pt starting at 23mm

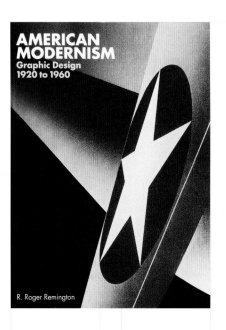

AMERICAN MODERNISM
Graphic Design
1920 to 1960

R. Roger Remington

Of this novel H. G. Wells wrote: *"I do not know how to express the admiration I feel for this wonderful book without seeming to be extravagant. I am not usually lavish with my praise, but indeed the book impresses me as among the very greatest novels I have ever read. It is wholly beautiful, it is saturated with wisdom and humor and tenderness."*

Growth of the Soil

KNUT HAMSUN

HISTORY LIBERTY
BENEDETTO CROCE

The mind and heart of love

five stories Willa Cather

CONTAINER CORPORATION OF AMERICA

MONTANA

ONE

CONTAINER CORPORATION OF AMERICA

Above left The French poster artist Jean Carlu lived in New York during World War II. He designed many advertisements and posters on behalf of the war effort. This ad for the Container Corporation of America was created in 1942. Entitled 'Repaying America's Riches', it represented the CCA's public service support in presenting one million pine tree seedlings to Florida farmers in terms of understandable imagery.

Above right This ad, designed by Paul Rand, ran in consumer magazines in the United States in 1946. It was the first ad in a long series in which each of the 48 United States was featured. The headline read: 'U.S. 48 States light the road to world peace and commerce.' The ad reflected the post-World War II optimism for peace and prosperity. Rand's visualization was characteristic in the simplified synthesis of illustration with graphic symbolic form.

talent – tenacity, diplomacy and salesmanship. It is no good to create a beautiful layout if disintegration sets in at any one of the important points of production.[7] In the postwar period, with the economy moving again, more and more Modernist designers were active in producing imaginative advertisements and receiving recognition for bringing fresh, design-oriented solutions to the world of marketing.

GRAPHIC DESIGN ACROSS AMERICA

Two prominent designers, Paul Rand and Bradbury Thompson, emerged during the war and made major contributions to the new direction in American graphic design. They shared an interest in bringing the formal ideas of the European avant-garde into their work at the same time as being firmly grounded in the realities of the American business scene.

Rand, a native New Yorker, worked through the 1940s at the Weintraub Advertising Agency, designing outstanding campaigns for Orbachs, Stafford Fabrics, Disney Hats and others. His covers for *Direction* magazine afforded the opportunity to explore new approaches in form and content interpretation. The covers show Rand's unique understanding of perceptual values, his

Above left Montana was the birth state of E. McKnight Kauffer. He had spent most of his career in England but participated in the Container Corporation of America's 48 States campaign with this ad for his home state in 1944. The CCA ad campaign featured a prominent artist or illustrator from each of the 48 states.

Above right Fernand Leger was a famous French artist who waited out World War II in New York. While he was in the U.S., art directors such as Charles Coiner asked Leger to produce work for Container Corporation of America's ad campaigns. This ad, from 1941, emphasized the fact that the CCA organization was a full-service packaging business. Leger also designed covers for *Fortune* magazine.

Overleaf Between 1947 and 1949, Paul Rand designed a series of ads for Disney Hats. In the campaign, each ad was different but was composed of similar elements, namely a hat, the outline of a figure, the company seal and the copy. This series showed Rand's ingenuity at presenting a visually uninteresting product line with creativity and visual interest.

Grids: Creative Solutions for Graphic Designers

Opposite This design was for the back page of a Futurist newspaper titled Futurismo. It was produced in 1918 by Mino Somenzi and was an example of how Modernist graphic design approaches could be used in creating a complex but powerful printed page in support of Futurism in Italy before World War II. This effect is achieved through the complex directional juxtapositions of small-text type, bold headline types and colour.

Above This page is from a small booklet designed by Kurt Schwitters in 1930 in an attempt to codify the principles of avant-garde graphic design and advertising. The booklet was in effect a manifesto in which a forceful message was presented to really standards in the way graphic design (elements) and advertising were made. Conceived as one of a series, the booklet included on its back cover a series of principles, entitled Typographic Topography , contributed by the Russian Constructivist designer El Lissitzky. Among his offerings from his publication Merz was 'The words in a printed page are seen and not heard.'

Overleaf Several avant-garde designers created dynamic advertisements for Pelikan Ink. This ad from 1924, designed by Kurt Schwitters, features dominant directional arrows to control the visual flow on the magazine page. Another Pelikan ink ad, by the Russian Constructivist El Lissitzky, can be seen on page 29.

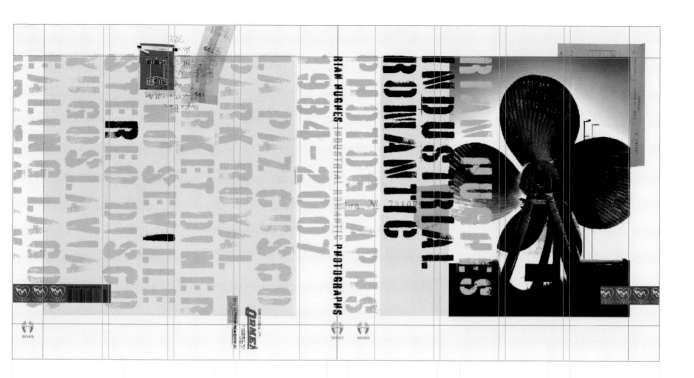

GRID SPECIFICATIONS

Page size (trimmed)	260 x 260mm
Top margin	25mm
Bottom margin	27mm
Outside margin	25mm
Inside margin	30mm
Number of columns	4
Gutter width	5mm
Extras	N/A

INDUSTRIAL ROMANTIC

Design: Rian Hughes at Device

Rian Hughes is best known as an illustrator, and a graphic and font designer, but this book focuses on his photographs. It was a challenge to develop a system that would accommodate images with such a variation in size and proportion. Hughes decided to use a square format for the book, which he found sensitive to both portrait and landscape images. His four-column grid had to be used flexibly. Hughes consistently aligned three sides of his photographs with the grid, but allowed one edge to break it, determined by the best crop and scale for that particular shot. He selected the images for each spread based on their relative size as well as their subject matter. The layout is then disrupted by the more randomly placed related ephemera.

GRID SPECIFICATIONS

Page size (trimmed)	250 x 250mm
Top margin	5mm
Bottom margin	5mm
Outside margin	5mm
Inside margin	5mm
Number of columns	10
Gutter width	2mm
Extras	10 horizontal fields

200% COTTON: NEW T-SHIRT GRAPHICS and
300% COTTON: MORE T-SHIRT GRAPHICS

Design: Agathe Jacquillat and Tomi Vollauschek at Fl@33

These image-based books contain over 1,000 illustrations each. The grid had to be flexible, provide consistency, and make the design process relatively systematic. Designers Agathe Jacquillat and Tomi Vollauschek developed a multicolumn grid with 10 horizontal fields. In *200%* dotted rules form threadlike outlines to frame and connect images and text, foregrounding the grid in a playful way, and making a subtle association with fashion and needlework. The brief for *300%* was to refresh the layout while maintaining the visual identity of the previous title in the series. Jacquillat and Vollauschek chose to exploit the versatility of the grid by introducing diagonals to the layout. The result is a lively reinterpretation of the previously used system.

Grids: Creative Solutions for Graphic Designers

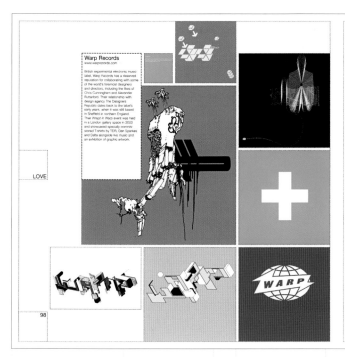

LOVE

98

Warp Records
www.warprecords.com

British experimental electronic music label, Warp Records has a deserved reputation for collaborating with some of the world's foremost designers and directors, including the likes of Chris Cunningham and Alexander Rutterford. Their relationship with design agency The Designers Republic dates back to the label's early years, when it was still based in Sheffield in northern England. Their *Warp in Warp* event was held in a London gallery space in 2003 and showcased specially commissioned T-shirts by TDR, Dan Sparkes and Delta alongside live music and an exhibition of graphic artwork.

One-Brand Inc.
www.usa-t.com

'At an early age we all write a literary masterpiece on our home state,' says New York-based designer Todd Wilcox, the brains behind all-American brand USA-T.com. This site allows people to create their own shirt, featuring either the icon or bird of any of the fifty American states. 'Home Sweet Home,' concludes Wilcox proudly.

99

134

135

108

109

Published in 2006 by
Laurence King Publishing
71 Great Russell Street
London WC1B 3BP
Tel: +44 020 7430 8850
Fax: +44 020 7430 8880
email: enquiries@laurenceking.co.uk
www.laurenceking.co.uk

Copyright © 2006
Laurence King Publishing

A catalogue record for this book is
available from the British Library.

ISBN 1 85669 491 7

Words: Helen Walters

Book design and cover illustration:
FL@33
www.flat33.com

Senior editor: Catherine Hall
Assistant editor: Andy Prince

Printed in China

300%
Cotton
More T-Shirt Graphics

Words: Helen Walters

Book design and cover illustration: FL@33

Laurence King Publishing

Intro

Love

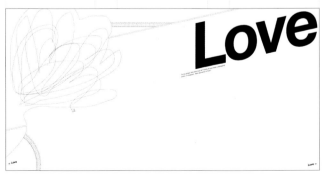

Grids: Creative Solutions for Graphic Designers

INTRODUCTION

'Take any form you please and repeat it at regular intervals and, as surely as recurrent sounds give rhythm or cadence, whether you want it or not, you have pattern.'

Lewis F. Day

This book is a collection of a number of contemporary surface patterns created between 2000 and 2005 by designers and artists from many different cultures and backgrounds.

The patterns have been achieved by a number of techniques, which include drawing, painting, collage, embroidery, appliqué, hand dyeing and screen printing. Many of the designs have been digitally manipulated. As this was a project facilitated almost entirely by e-mail and digitalized images, this is not surprising. What has been surprising is the range and variety of initiating ideas, as outlined by the artists themselves. These run from 'Mary Poppins Dissected' to 'The Cornish Seascape' to 'Chaos Theory'! I have included the artists' own comments on their inspiration and content wherever possible.

The patterns themselves have been chosen subjectively by me for their perceived qualities of beauty and balance, their use of colour and overall aesthetic appeal. They have been grouped into families following a contemporary understanding of the traditional surface design categories, and I have also arranged the patterns so that they fall in a definite and, I trust, pleasing colour order within each category.

006

040

100

Grids: Creative Solutions for Graphic Designers

INTRODUCTION

'Take any form you please and repeat it at regular intervals and, as surely as recurrent sounds give rhythm or cadence, whether you want it or not, you have pattern.'

Lewis F. Day

This book is a collection of a number of contemporary surface patterns created between 2000 and 2005 by designers and artists from many different cultures and backgrounds.

The patterns have been achieved by a number of techniques, which include drawing, painting, collage, embroidery, appliqué, hand dyeing and screen printing. Many of the designs have been digitally manipulated. As this was a project facilitated almost entirely by e-mail and digitalized images, this is not surprising. What has been surprising is the range and variety of initiating ideas, as outlined by the artists themselves. These run from 'Mary Poppins Dissected' to 'The Cornish Seascape' to 'Chaos Theory'! I have included the artists' own comments on their inspiration and content wherever possible.

The patterns themselves have been chosen subjectively by me for their perceived qualities of beauty and balance, their use of colour and overall aesthetic appeal. They have been grouped into families following a contemporary understanding of the traditional surface design categories, and I have also arranged the patterns so that they fall in a definite and, I trust, pleasing colour order within each category.

006

PATTERNS: NEW SURFACE DESIGN

Design: Agathe Jacquillat and Tomi Vollauschek at Fl@33

Coming up with a system that would accommodate examples of elaborate and visually rich pattern making sensitively was a challenge for designers Agathe Jacquillat and Tomi Vollauschek. They had little editorial control over the selection or grouping of the images, which was determined by the author. But, their highly flexible grid allowed them to vary the scale and area used for each example to ensure that the visual relationships between patterns were sympathetic, and potential clashes between designs could be avoided. The page is divided into 12 vertical columns and 17 horizontal fields, with a folio, running foot, and caption zone at the bottom of the page.

GRID SPECIFICATIONS

Page size (trimmed)	170 x 240mm
Top margin	8mm
Bottom margin	16mm
Outside margin	8mm
Inside margin	8mm
Number of columns	12
Gutter width	5mm
Extras	17 horizontal fields

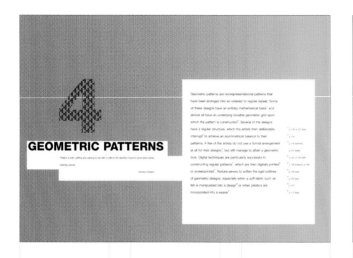

4
GEOMETRIC PATTERNS

Pattern is both uplifting and calming to live with; it reflects the repetition found in nature and cosmic inspiring stories.

Dominic Crinson

Geometric patterns are nonrepresentational patterns that have been arranged into an ordered or regular repeat. Some of these designs have an entirely mathematical basis[1] and almost all have an underlying invisible geometric grid upon which the pattern is constructed[2]. Several of the designs have a regular structure, which the artists then deliberately interrupt[3] to achieve an asymmetrical balance to their patterns. A few of the artists do not use a formal arrangement at all for their designs[4], but still manage to attain a geometric look. Digital techniques are particularly successful in constructing regular patterns[5], which are then digitally printed[6] or screenprinted[7]. Texture serves to soften the rigid outlines of geometric designs, especially when a soft fabric such as felt is manipulated into a design[8] or when plastics are incorporated into a weave[9].

[1] 118 and 121 Stefan Hanser
[2] 154
[3] 172 Keira Marsh
[4] 122 and 125 Keira Marsh
[5] 126 Wendy Graham
[6] 168 Emily Alston
[7] 132 Wendy Graham
[8] 147
[9] 172 Keira Marsh

1 Eugene Van Veldhoven ... Interwine images of pale pink, magenta and yellow have been produced in this fabric sample. The artist elaborates: 'two different coloured layers of crepe voile have been slit by a laser, creating many different crinques of the two colours.' 15 Henn Jess ... Concentric circles and herringbone feature in this computer-generated pattern. The artist remarks: 'Based on pebbles, the circles in this pattern represent the apex of the links that had been made by pressure and time.' 3 Rachel Moore ... Grey, white and red tones of pale sand been combined to produce a pattern of three-dimensional boxes in this hand screenprinted textile. 4 Dominic Crinson ... A simple digitally produced tile with sparkling highlights. The artist observes: 'Pattern is both uplifting and calming to live with.' It reflects the repetition found in nature and creates inspiring stories.

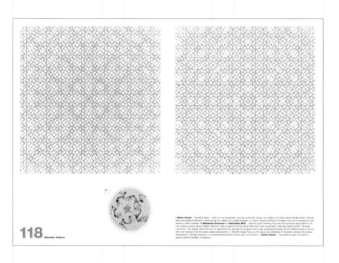

1 Stefan Hanser ... The artist states: 'I work out non-expressive, concrete continually, designs and patterns by using mathematically raised methods again and graphical elements, which are set any relation to a graphical pattern, by colors reduced aesthetic information that can be perceived by the viewer by active analysis.' 5 Bethsabée Grossman ... to Materialise MGX ... Selective Laser Sintering (SLS) was the technique responsible for this truly amazing, tightly three-omitted 'Quintrino' with its interconnecting spirals that twist in and around each other, like reading starfish. The artist comments: 'The design marks the root of a series that can anymore its sculpture link in side, progressing through the ten Platonic solids to the four and multi-musical of the familiar sided dodecahedron. In this 3D shape Platu saw the nature and wholeness of the entire universe, the spiritual counterpoint. This tight structure is a household assortment of that unity, the Quantrin.' 3 Stefan Hanser ... 'The pattern is part of a series of graphic patterns entitled 'interference'.

7 Emily Alston ... Circles of lace, resembling snowflakes, have been arranged into a pattern for a large format wall covering. God's lace circle is 'diamond' unlike snowflakes which grow in a fractal manner and are more orderly alike.

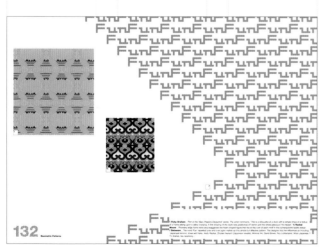

1 Vicky Graham ... Part of the 'Mary Poppins Dissected' series. The artist comments: 'This is a silhouette of a clock with a simple stripe of a status of a frame sitting upon a yellow inisiping. A fine drawing of the clock was positioned of narror and the whole piece put into repeat.' 6 Rachel Moore ... Rounded edge forms echo and exaggerate the repeat patterns of the heart-shaped figure that lie at the core of this motif. 7 Deleware ... The motif 'Fun' repeated over and over again melted on this simple but effective pattern. The designer lists her influences as including: 'Japanese kimonos, Arais and Marie, Andy Warhol, Shusen-kiainch Kayasama [installation, William], life, David Bowie, Roy Lichtenstein, Miuki Uteamaro, TV dramas, tea ceremony.'

1 Keira Marsh ... Twisted foil large flare beads used to make plot of the welt in this unusual needlewoven fabric inspired by Cubhidm. 15 Keira Marsh ... An open weave in black and metal-liked dash yarns make up this sample. The artist comments: 'I developed this piece from an idea of a fifties-web macabre with illustration — which uses repeated reasonable lozengle shapes.' 4 Keira Marsh ... This textile in this woven textile have been created by a method of patterning and spacing the warp. 16 Keira Marsh ... The restructure in this woven textile offers. 17 Giovanna Cotton ... The eye-catching design is made up of undulating zig-zags of white 'S' shapes on black, which create a visually mesmerizing pattern.

210 Organic Patterns

216 Organic Patterns

CONTRIBUTORS

238

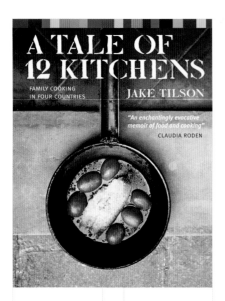

A TALE OF 12 KITCHENS

FAMILY COOKING IN FOUR COUNTRIES

JAKE TILSON

"An enchantingly evocative memoir of food and cooking"
CLAUDIA RODEN

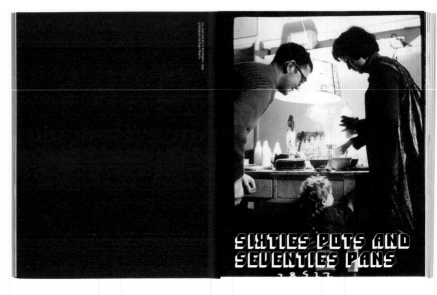

SIXTIES POTS AND SEVENTIES PANS

DON'T GO TO ANY TROUBLE BACKSTREET COUSCOUS

COUSCOUS
BROCHETTES
MERGUEZ
TARTINES BEURRÉES
CROQUE MONSIEUR

A dish that encourages interpretation and invention. I assemble mine with the assimilated memories of smoke-filled Tunisian restaurants in Paris and three memorable meals in a frenzied visit to Morocco in my youth. In Paris they tend towards the separation of the meat from the stew. This becomes an inspiring triad of tastes and texture – soft, dry couscous grains, crisp roast meat accompanied by the wet vegetable stew. Couscous is the name for both the semolina grain and the dish itself. Serve with roasted meat, chicken, lamb, fish or sausages.
Serves 8

5 carrots, sliced in rounds	*spices*
5 courgettes, sliced in rounds	1 stick of cinnamon
3 onions, roughly chopped	1 teaspoon ground cumin
3 large cabbage leaves, shredded	1 teaspoon ground coriander
3 cups chickpeas, precooked or canned	1 teaspoon ground ginger
600ml (1 pint) of chicken stock	1 teaspoon freshly ground cumin seeds
3 cloves of garlic, chopped	10 threads of saffron
3 tablespoons of tomato purée and/or	15 sprigs of fresh coriander, tied in a bunch
1 400g (14oz), can of tomatoes, finely mashed	15 sprigs of fresh parsley, tied in a bunch

Vegetable stew – quick method
To achieve a backstreet Parisian-Tunisian style vegetable stew, adopt a nonchalant approach. Put all the ingredients in a large pan, cover with water and simmer for 30 minutes. Done. Serve with couscous grains and roasted or grilled meats.

Variations
You could add harder root vegetables first and softer ones towards the end of cooking for a more consistent bite. Some cooks first fry the spices, onions and garlic until transparent, before adding the remaining ingredients. The key items are carrots, courgettes and chickpeas. Improvise with chicory, shredded cabbage, diced squash or even a stray potato.

Couscous grains
I use a medium wholegrain couscous from our local Iranian store. Barley couscous is also good, with a nutty flavour. I use a quick method for preparing the couscous grains taught to me by a Parisian friend. A medium-grain couscous is easier to cook than fine.
Serves 8

2 cups of medium-grain couscous	1 tablespoon butter
salt	30 sultanas for decoration
saffron (optional)	

Put the couscous grains into a bowl with a few strands of saffron and a little salt. Gently pour boiling water onto the couscous until the water just breaks the surface of the grains, do not mix it. Leave to soak for 20 minutes. Melt a knob of butter in a large pan. The bowl of soaked couscous grains will appear to be a solid mass. With a fork gently plough away the top layer of grains off into the hot buttered pan. Slowly loosen off all of the grains into the pan. Heat through, stirring with a flat-ended wooden spoon for a few minutes. You can cover the pan and reheat later.
    Heap the cooked couscous in a pyramid on a warmed round plate and dot a ring of sultanas around the edge.

Accompaniment
Any roasted meat or fish forms the final point of the couscous triad. Country chicken (p 82), *agnello scottadito* without the sage (p 65). Merguez sausages, grilled fish or fried sardines. A leg of lamb rubbed with cumin, coriander and teaspoon of harissa, then roasted on a bed of outer cabbage leaves sprinkled with caraway seeds. A *couscous royale* in Paris is a mixed platter of chicken, lamb and merguez.

To serve
Transfer the stew to a deep serving bowl with a ladle. Each plate requires a heap of couscous grains, meat and a ladle of vegetable stew. Throughout the meal the couscous grains seem never to diminish on your plate if replenished with enough liquid stew.

GRID SPECIFICATIONS

Page size (trimmed)	250 x 196mm
Top margin	11mm
Bottom margin	11mm
Outside margin	15mm
Inside margin	15mm
Number of columns	6
Gutter width	3mm
Extras	N/A

A TALE OF 12 KITCHENS

Design: Jake Tilson at Jake Tilson Studio

As author, designer, photographer, and cook, every aspect of this book is the creation of passionate cook, and artist, Jake Tilson. It provides a distinctive multisensory perspective on seeing and tasting food, from the way it is grown, packaged, and bought, to how it is cooked and remembered. The underlying structure of the book had to support an evocative memoir and a functional cookery book. The grid divides the page into four equal columns and two narrower columns, plus horizontal fields. Although Tilson's recipe layouts are conventional, eclectic combinations of photos, fonts, and ephemera surround them. His goal was to share how much fun food can be, and to produce a guide for his daughter on the significance of cooking and eating in the life of their family.

BEAUTY PACKAGE

FOREWORD

ROSS LOVEGROVE

Sitting here in my London studio, in the tranquility of the early morning before my assistants arrive, I look around me at a space filled with organic shapes, nature's forms, and modern technology all living in a certain harmony together. This precious silence allows my mind to wander, contemplating the future and the role that design will play in its success or failure.

DESIGN THIS DAY: 8 DECADES OF INFLUENTIAL DESIGN
Design: Steve Watson, Ben Graham, Jason Gómez, and Bryan Mamaril at Turnstyle

This limited-edition book was produced to commemorate industrial design company Teague's 80th anniversary. Designers Steve Watson, Ben Graham, Jason Gómez, and Bryan Mamaril wanted the graphic design to reflect the attention to detail characteristic of Teague's design solutions. The typography and navigational devices are clean and systematic, but allow for subtle changes between sections. Reminiscent of some of the complex grids developed by the Swiss designers of the 1950s and 1960s, their 12-column grid is divided into 20 horizontal fields. The book is not just a showcase of Teague's finished work—it gives context by drawing on their initial ideas and methods of working, as well as showing the work of their design heroes. This provided an opportunity for Turnstyle to vary the visual pace of the book and introduce different paper stocks to make this a tactile as well as a visual experience.

GRID SPECIFICATIONS

Page size (trimmed)	228.6 x 304.8mm
Top margin	9.525mm
Bottom margin	9.525mm
Outside margin	9.525mm
Inside margin	19.05mm
Number of columns	12
Gutter width	4.064mm
Extras	Baseline grid, 0.706mm starting at 9.525mm; 20 horizontal fields

Client
Samsung Electronics

→ 04.1
Portable Digital Projector

The compact and ultra portable projector was designed specifically for the highly mobile professional. Created to fit easily into today's busy schedule—not to mention a small bag or purse—the Samsung Portable Digital Projector is no larger than a digital camera. Utilizing laser diode technology to offer an integrated and seamless display experience, users interact with and control the extremely versatile projector via their mobile phone.

Client
Nike

→ 04.2
Portable Sports Audio

Teague worked with Nike's in-house team on all design aspects of this lightweight, rugged, and sophisticated family of products. Designed for the serious athlete, the MP3 Run's wireless features include a distance and speed sensor, as well as skip-free audio and FM radio that keeps athletes in tune with their music and their workout. The complementary MP3 CD's shock-resistant technology, no-look control belt, and strobe light all cater to the athlete who wants an uninterrupted workout experience.

Date	Award	Award
2004	2005 iF	2006 IDEA Silver

Date
2005

Grids: Creative Solutions for Graphic Designers

GIAN LORENZO
BERNINI
Apollo and Daphne
1622-1625
marble

I. THE
    MYTH
   OF ER

In the tremendous vision of transmigration which closes Plato's *Republic,* the dead are able to choose their fate in their future lives: Socrates describes how a warrior called Er was taken for dead and entered the other world, but came back to life on his funeral pyre; after he had returned from the other world, he described how he saw there, in "a certain demonic place," the souls of Homeric heroes taking on their next existence—in the form of a new daimon. The dead were told, "A demon will not select you, but you will choose a demon. Let him who gets the first lot make the first choice of a life to which he will be bound by necessity."[1] As Er watches the redistribution of lives after death, he recognizes Orpheus who chooses to become a swan, Ajax who singles out the life of a lion, and Agamemnon who decides to become an eagle. The heroes' future metamorphoses in some ways correspond to their past character, sometimes ironically. Atalanta, the swift runner, chooses to become a male athlete, for example; Epeius, who made the Trojan horse, opts to become a female

53

META
MOMOR
PHOHOS
IS S

MARINA warner

I. THE
MYTH
OF ER

In the tremendous vision of transmigration which closes Plato's *Republic*, the dead are able to choose their fate in their future lives: Socrates describes how a warrior called Er was taken for dead and entered the other world, but came back to life on his funeral pyre; after he had returned from the other world, he described how he saw there, in "a certain demonic place," the souls of Homeric heroes taking on their next existence—in the form of a new daimon. The dead were told, "A demon will not select you, but you will choose a demon. Let him who gets the first lot make the first choice of a life to which he will be bound by necessity."[1] As Er watches the redistribution of lives after death, he recognizes Orpheus who chooses to become a swan, Ajax who singles out the life of a lion, and Agamemnon who decides to become an eagle. The heroes' future metamorphoses in some ways correspond to their past character, sometimes ironically. Atalanta, the swift runner, chooses to become a male athlete, for example; Epeius, who made the Trojan horse, opts to become a female

GIAN LORENZO
BERNINI
Apollo and Daphne
1622|1625
marble

GRID SPECIFICATIONS

Page size (trimmed)	152.4 x 203.2mm
Top margin	19.05mm
Bottom margin	12.7mm
Outside margin	19.05mm
Inside margin	12.7mm
Number of columns	9
Gutter width	3.81mm
Extras	N/A

UNEASY NATURE

Design: Eric Heiman, Amber Reed, and Madhavi Jagdish at Volume Inc.

This exhibition catalog was produced for Weatherspoon Art Museum. The designers explored ideas of mutation by juxtaposing the natural and the unnatural in their design. They started with the cover, on which all the images from the show are overlaid digitally to create a single composite image. The typographic grid uses the golden section, however, the designers break this grid repeatedly, with various typographic mutations that often bleed off the pages. The body text changes from sans serif to serif throughout the essays, and on the whole, text and image are not integrated. The cover and essay pages are printed in two colors on uncoated cream stock, while the images are contained within a full-color section on coated white paper.

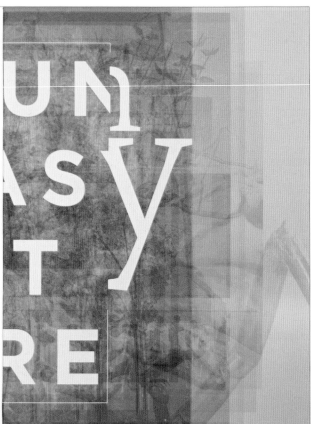

LEE BUL
BRYAN CROCKETT
ROXY PAINE
PATRICIA PICCININI
ALYSON SHOTZ
JENNIFER STEINKAMP

UN
EASy
NAT
URE

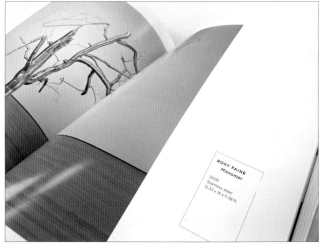

ROXY PAINE
Misnomer

2005
Stainless steel
12.33 × 16 × 11.58 ft.

Grids: Creative Solutions for Graphic Designers

CONTENTS

IIT McCormick Center, Chicago (1998)

Michael Dulin

There is an positive change to the grounds of Illinois Institute of Technology - a welcome send to attract all the faculty, staff and students who have had to endure the deafening rattle of the passing Chicago Transit Authority trains for decades. As with all other buildings on campus, this one has been in the making for many years: the Office of Metropolitan Architecture (OMA) has completed the McCormick Tribune campus center. Rem Koolhaas' first stand-alone building in the United States, one of the first new buildings on the IIT campus in over 20 years. With an emphasis on bold rationalism, the dramatic role that combines the old academic architecture and the world-famous campus, perhaps.

The winning entry submitted by oma for the 1998 competition was a huge surprise from the very simplicity of the original structure - a departure that created an accessible community within the centre of the campus's diehard followers of Mies van der Rohe, who designed the original campus. Rem asked about the naysayers who had challenged his design, Koolhaas responded by reckoning to facts on the structure actually untenably rises; the entryway that had been an old central core, the entryway was widening to put the dramatic increase in thwarted enrolment in the 1980s and early 1990s and the ensuing loss of density that left the campus feeling lonely and somewhat dangerous. Buildings were a thumper, the palm-plant auditorium and the overall layout of the lecture was one that was one that had been charged not just with designing a new building, but also with improving what Koolhaas himself referred to as the damned site of the Mies campus.

The final product certainly aims to be an architectural statement and it is more left to By some

as the original competition model suggested. While approached from the Mies corridor, or, as the McCormick Center reads as a continuous building topped with a 535-foot long stainless-steel tube. The tube has naturally become the bedpost, yet, it is for utilitarian sound abatement. The way in which the student buildings between the dorms and the classroom buildings to create the bespoke nature, which are greater programmatic elements must be correlated. Though not reading entries, its rigor and innovation anticipated transitorily assigned to spaces, interchangeable locations within the plan. In fact, the main auditorium was rotated 90 degrees and an entire million with to was intervened with only minimal adjustments to the base floor plan.

The student paths were not essentially the same throughout the development of the project. Jeffrey Johnson, the project manager who oversaw the completion of the building, explained that the primary goal was to insert the urban experience within the building. By re-energising the core of the campus, by making it live and between two storeys. The building is designed in such a way as to exploit how the best of centum encounters can genuinely express in a busy urban area. The angles of which the pathways intersect seem to suggest an urgency of movement: either between corridors or to a most swift frenzy, movements that wouldn't necessarily exist in a milder glass box. This was paramount in order to develop the sense of density that had previously been missing from the campus. By articulating the movement of students, and not simply framing space for them to move to and from, the building has a

Government Buildings

Axel Schultes/Charlotte Frank
(Berlin, Germany)
German Chancellery Building,
Berlin, Germany
Invited Competition 1994
Completed 2001

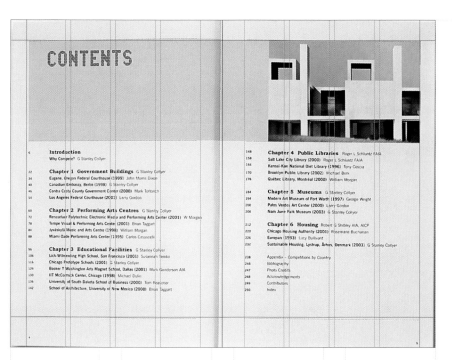

CONTENTS

GRID SPECIFICATIONS

Page size (trimmed)	240 x 164mm
Top margin	15mm
Bottom margin	22mm
Outside margin	12mm
Inside margin	17mm
Number of columns	1, 2, or 4
Gutter width	4mm
Extras	N/A

AP ARCHITECTURE IN PRACTICE

Design: Christian Küsters at CHK Design

Christian Küsters developed an accessible and user-friendly system for this series of practice-based architectural books. The design is based on a single matrix that forms the basis of the logotype, and is the inspiration for the headline font, as well as the grid system of the book. The grid defines areas for a large heading zone at the top, one wide column and related information to the left, or two columns of continuous text. Küsters wanted the books to feel like handbooks, and designed the font Matrix specifically for this series. His choice of secondary fonts included New Gothic, because it is spatially economical and architectural in feel, contrasted with Bookman Old Style.

Identities

68

GRID SPECIFICATIONS

Page size (trimmed)	210 x 170mm
Top margin	5mm
Bottom margin	5mm
Outside margin	5mm
Inside margin	15mm
Number of columns	6
Gutter width	5mm
Extras	Baseline grid 5mm; 6 horizontal fields

365 PAGES

Design: BB/Saunders

Every week, members of design and branding consultancy
BB/Saunders produce a diary for inclusion on its website.
The brief is open; it might be a map of somebody's last seven days
or a manifesto calling to save the world. The initial idea behind *365
Pages* was to catalog these and create a journal of diaries. Based
on the assumption that designers love to doodle in sketchbooks,
BB/Saunders went on to create a book that included inventive and
unusual multicolumn and field-based grids as backgrounds to the
pages—the objective was to encourage readers to record their own
daily experiences, observations, or thoughts. Using its in-house
technical drafting grids as a starting point, 12 new grids were
created for this book.

323

235

332

334

2yrs_mar'04_mar'06

1

2 3

14 15

4 5

16 17

12 13

18 19

22

23

32

33

24

25

34

35

30

31

36

37

JORGE JORGE DESIGN IDENTITY

Design: Jorge Jorge at Jorge Jorge Design

Jorge Jorge's aim was to create a simple and contemporary identity that would work across a range of graphic applications and formats, and communicate his personality and potential to clients. He achieved this through economic means; the diagonal rules and use of limited color distinguish a considered and minimal layout. Although grids are used most prevalently in multipage documents, they can also be used very effectively across a range of related single-page items. Here Jorge Jorge's grid ensures consistency. It determines hanging heights and alignments across each element of the stationery.

Fax

For: Dr. João Soares
Company: Brand Y
Fax nº: 225 876 987
Subject: Something

From: Jorge Jorge
Pages: 1/2
Date: 22/02/07
Reply to: JorgeJorge / 225 899 645

JorgeJorgeDesigner

Porto, 14 Janeiro 2007

Olá João Soares!

Lorem ipsum dolor sit amet, consectetuer adipiscing elit, sed diam nonummy nibh euismod tincidunt ut laoreet dolore magna aliquam erat volutpat. Ut wisi enim ad minim veniam, quis nostrud exerci tation ullamcorper suscipit lobortis nisl ut aliquip ex ea commodo consequat. Duis autem vel eum iriure dolor in hendrerit in vulputate velit esse molestie consequat, vel illum dolore eu feugiat nulla facilisis at vero eros et accumsan et iusto odio dignissim qui blandit praesent luptatum zzril delenit augue duis dolore te feugait nulla facilisi. Lorem ipsum dolor sit amet, consectetuer adipiscing elit, sed diam nonummy nibh euismod tincidunt ut laoreet dolore magna erat volutpat. Ut wisi enim ad minim veniam, quis nostrud exerci tation ullamcorper suscipit lobortis nisl ut aliquip ex ea commodo consequat.

Duis autem vel eum iriure dolor in hendrerit in vulputate velit esse molestie consequat, vel illum dolore eu feugiat nulla facilisis at vero eros et accumsan et iusto odio dignissim qui blandit praesent luptatum zzril delenit augue duis dolore te feugait nulla facilisi. Nam liber tempor cum soluta nobis eleifend option congue nihil imperdiet doming id quod mazim placerat facer possim assum. Lorem ipsum dolor sit amet, consectetuer adipiscing elit, sed diam nonummy nibh euismod tincidunt ut laoreet dolore magna aliquam erat volut

Aguardo contacto seu!
Cumprimentos,

Jorge Jorge

+351 934 201 420
mail@jorgejorge.com
www.jorgejorge.com

Internal Memo   Subject: New Briefing

JorgeJorgeDesigner

Subject 01

Lorem ipsum dolor sit amet, consectetuer adipiscing elit, sed diam nonummy nibh euismod tincidunt ut laoreet dolore magna aliquam erat volutpat. Ut wisi enim ad minim veniam, quis nostrud exerci tation ullamcorper suscipit lobortis nisl ut aliquip ex ea commodo consequat. Duis autem vel eum iriure dolor in hendrerit in vulputate velit esse molestie consequat, vel illum dolore eu feugiat nulla facilisis at vero eros et accumsan et iusto odio dignissim qui blandit praesent luptatum zzril delenit augue duis dolore te feugait nulla facilisi. Lorem ipsum dolor sit amet, consectetuer adipiscing elit, sed diam nonummy nibh euismod tincidunt ut laoreet dolore magna aliquam erat volutpat. Ut wisi enim ad minim veniam, quis nostrud exerci tation ullamcorper suscipit lobortis nisl ut aliquip ex ea commodo consequat.

Subject 02

Duis autem vel eum iriure dolor in hendrerit in vulputate velit esse molestie consequat, vel illum dolore eu feugiat nulla facilisis at vero eros et accumsan et iusto odio dignissim qui blandit praesent luptatum zzril delenit augue duis dolore te feugait nulla facilisi. Nam liber tempor cum soluta nobis eleifend option congue nihil imperdiet doming id quod mazim placerat facer possim assum. Lorem ipsum dolor sit amet, consectetuer adipiscing elit, sed diam nonummy nibh euismod tincidunt ut laoreet dolore magna aliquam erat volut

+351 934 201 420
mail@jorgejorge.com
www.jorgejorge.com

Subject:

Jorge Jorge Designer

Porto, 14 Janeiro 2007

Olá João Soares!

Lorem ipsum dolor sit amet, consectetuer adipiscing elit, sed diam nonummy nibh euismod tincidunt ut laoreet dolore magna aliquam erat volutpat. Ut wisi enim ad minim veniam, quis nostrud exerci tation ullamcorper suscipit lobortis nisl ut aliquip ex ea commodo consequat. Duis autem vel eum iriure dolor in hendrerit in vulputate velit esse molestie consequat, vel illum dolore eu feugiat nulla facilisis at vero eros et accumsan et iusto odio dignissim qui blandit praesent luptatum zzril delenit augue duis dolore te feugait nulla facilisi. Lorem ipsum dolor sit amet, consectetuer adipiscing elit, sed diam nonummy nibh euismod tincidunt ut laoreet dolore magna aliquam erat volutpat. Ut wisi enim ad minim veniam, quis nostrud exerci tation ullamcorper suscipit lobortis nisl ut aliquip ex ea commodo consequat.

Duis autem vel eum iriure dolor in hendrerit in vulputate velit esse molestie consequat, vel illum dolore eu feugiat nulla facilisis at vero eros et accumsan et iusto odio dignissim qui blandit praesent luptatum zzril delenit augue duis dolore te feugait nulla facilisi. Nam liber tempor cum soluta nobis eleifend option congue nihil imperdiet doming id quod mazim placerat facer possim assum. Lorem ipsum dolor sit amet, consectetuer adipiscing elit, sed diam nonummy nibh euismod tincidunt ut laoreet dolore magna aliquam erat volut

Aguardo contacto seu!

Cumprimentos,

Jorge Jorge

+351 934 201 420
mail@jorgejorge.com
www.jorgejorge.com

Subject:

Jorge·Jorge·Designer

Porto, 14 Janeiro 2007

Olá João Soares!

Lorem ipsum dolor sit amet, consectetuer adipiscing elit, sed diam nonummy nibh euismod tincidunt ut laoreet dolore magna aliquam erat volutpat. Ut wisi enim ad minim veniam, quis nostrud exerci tation ullamcorper suscipit lobortis nisl ut aliquip ex ea commodo consequat. Duis autem vel eum iriure dolor in hendrerit in vulputate velit esse molestie consequat, vel illum dolore eu feugiat nulla facilisis at vero eros et accumsan et iusto odio dignissim qui blandit praesent luptatum zzril delenit augue duis dolore te feugait nulla facilisi. Lorem ipsum dolor sit amet, consectetuer adipiscing elit, sed diam nonummy nibh euismod tincidunt ut laoreet dolore magna aliquam erat volutpat. Ut wisi enim ad minim veniam, quis nostrud exerci tation ullamcorper suscipit lobortis nisl ut aliquip ex ea commodo consequat.

Duis autem vel eum iriure dolor in hendrerit in vulputate velit esse molestie consequat, vel illum dolore eu feugiat nulla facilisis at vero eros et accumsan et iusto odio dignissim qui blandit praesent luptatum zzril delenit augue duis dolore te feugait nulla facilisi. Nam liber tempor cum soluta nobis eleifend option congue nihil imperdiet doming id quod mazim placerat facer possim assum. Lorem ipsum dolor sit amet, consectetuer adipiscing elit, sed diam nonummy nibh euismod tincidunt ut laoreet dolore magna aliquam erat volut

Aguardo contacto seu!

Cumprimentos,

Jorge Jorge

+351 934 201 420
mail@jorgejorge.com
www.jorgejorge.com

GRID SPECIFICATIONS

Page size (trimmed)	Card: 850 x 550mm
	Letterhead: 210 x 297mm
	Envelope: 110 x 220mm
Top margin	Card: 90mm
	Letterhead: 270mm
	Envelope: 350mm
Bottom margin	Card: 90mm
	Letterhead: 250mm
	Envelope: 350mm
Outside margin	Card: 9mm
	Letterhead: 27mm
	Envelope: 35mm
Inside margin	Card: 9mm
	Letterhead: 25mm
	Envelope: 35mm
Number of columns	Card: 4
	Letterhead: 5
	Envelope: 5
Gutter width	N/A
Extras	Card and envelope: 9 horizontal fields
	Letterhead: 20 horizontal fields

106_107

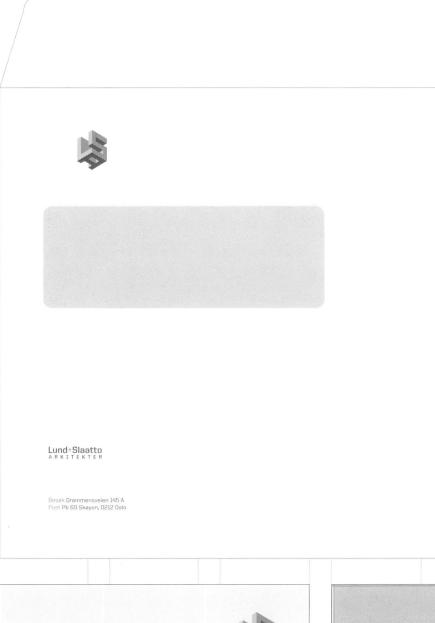

Lund+Slaatto
ARKITEKTER

Besøk Drammensveien 145 A
Post Pb 69 Skøyen, 0212 Oslo

Espen Pedersen
Sivilarkitekt MNLA / Partner

Besøk Drammensveien 145 A
Post Pb 69 Skøyen, 0212 Oslo

Dir +47 22 12 29 15
Mob +47 90 72 24 25
Email pedersen@lsa.no

Tel +47 22 12 29 00
Fax +47 22 12 29 99
Web www.lsa.no

Lund+Slaatto
ARKITEKTER

Espen Pedersen
Sivilarkitekt MNLA / Partner

Besøk Drammensveien 145 A
Post Pb 69 Skøyen, 0212 Oslo

Dir +47 22 12 29 15
Mob +47 90 72 24 25
Email pedersen@lsa.no

Tel +47 22 12 29 00
Fax +47 22 12 29 99
Web www.lsa.no

Lund+Slaatto
ARKITEKTER

GRID SPECIFICATIONS

Page size (trimmed)	Envelope: 228 x 161mm
	Card: 45.5 x 89mm
Top margin	Envelope: 4mm/Card: 0.5mm
Bottom margin	Envelope: 14mm/Card: 0.5mm
Outside margin	Envelope: 15mm/Card: 0.5mm
Inside margin	Envelope: 8mm/Card: 0.5mm
Number of columns	Envelope: 6/Card: 3
Gutter width	Envelope: 0.5mm/Card: 0.5mm
Extras	Base unit—landscape rectangle with a ratio of 2:1; baseline grid, 7pt; Envelope: 9 horizontal fields/ Card: 3 horizontal fields

LUND+SLAATTO STATIONERY

Design: Karl Martin Saetren at Mission Design

Mission Design developed this identity for leading Norwegian architects Lund+Slaatto. The pared down, clean design reflects the attention to detail and architectural style for which the client is known. The layout is based on a grid using fields that have a ratio of 2:1. To ensure consistency between small items, such as business cards, and larger pieces of print, this proportion is used in all the grids, although the overall size of each field does change. For large items, more fields are added to the overall grid. In this way the grid works across a range of scales and formats.

DAMIAN HEINISCH PHOTOGRAPHER

DAMIAN MICHAL HEINISCH
GRENSEVEIEN 11F
0571 OSLO, NORWAY
TLF +47 45 02 43 71
CONTACT@DAMIAN-HEINISCH.COM
WWW.DAMIAN-HEINISCH
ORG.NR. 983 587 305

01 —

02 —

GRID SPECIFICATIONS

Page size (trimmed)	210 x 297mm
Top margin	7.5mm
Bottom margin	8mm
Outside margin	N/A
Inside margin	N/A
Number of columns	34
Gutter width	1mm
Extras	Baseline grid, 24pt

DAMIAN HEINISCH STATIONERY
Design: Karl Martin Saetren at Mission Design

Most grids need both horizontal and vertical subdivisions, but this identity, for photographer Damian Heinisch, uses just a series of horizontal stripes that relate to the body height of the type. The smallest type equates to this unit of measurement and fits within the height of one of the grid's units, while the larger type fits within two. The muted color palette and strict systematic design create a distinctive look, while the dark and controlled atmosphere the design exudes echoes the stark and graphic photographs of the client.

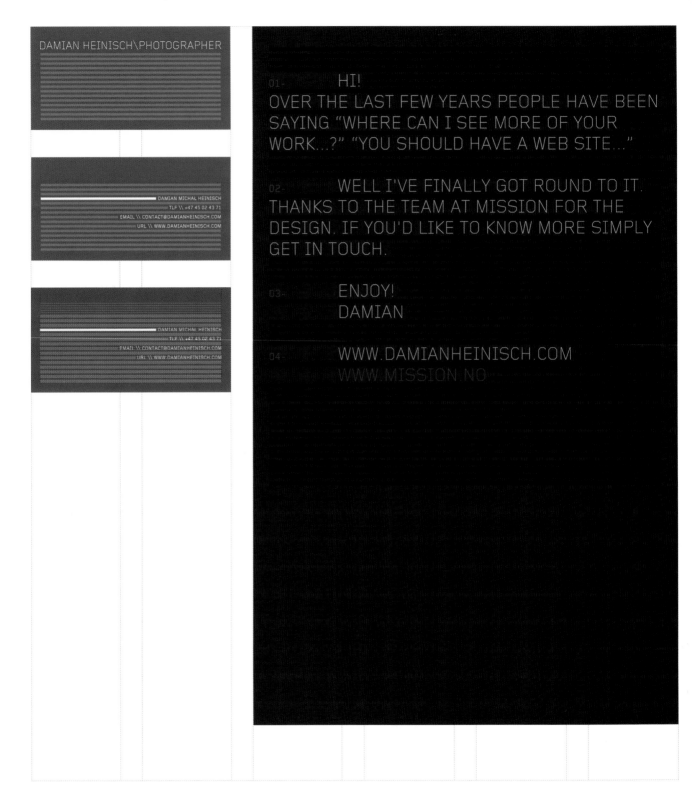

DAMIAN HEINISCH\PHOTOGRAPHER

DAMIAN MICHAŁ HEINISCH
TLF \\ +47 45 02 43 71
EMAIL \\ CONTACT@DAMIANHEINISCH.COM
URL \\ WWW.DAMIANHEINISCH.COM

DAMIAN MICHAŁ HEINISCH
TLF \\ +47 45 02 43 71
EMAIL \\ CONTACT@DAMIANHEINISCH.COM
URL \\ WWW.DAMIANHEINISCH.COM

01-   HI!
OVER THE LAST FEW YEARS PEOPLE HAVE BEEN
SAYING "WHERE CAN I SEE MORE OF YOUR
WORK...?" "YOU SHOULD HAVE A WEB SITE..."

02-   WELL I'VE FINALLY GOT ROUND TO IT.
THANKS TO THE TEAM AT MISSION FOR THE
DESIGN. IF YOU'D LIKE TO KNOW MORE SIMPLY
GET IN TOUCH.

03-   ENJOY!
DAMIAN

04-   WWW.DAMIANHEINISCH.COM
WWW.MISSION.NO

HI!

OVER THE LAST FEW YEARS PEOPLE HAVE BEEN SAYING "WHERE CAN I SEE MORE OF YOUR WORK...?" "YOU SHOULD HAVE A WEB SITE..."

WELL I'VE FINALLY GOT ROUND TO IT THANKS TO THE TEAM AT MISSION FOR THE DESIGN. IF YOU'D LIKE TO KNOW MORE SIMPLY GET IN TOUCH.

ENJOY!
DAMIAN

WWW.DAMIANHEINISCH.COM
WWW.MISSION.NO

GRID SPECIFICATIONS

Page size (trimmed)	176.4 x 282.2mm
Top margin	8.8mm
Bottom margin	91.72mm
Outside margin	7.05mm
Inside margin	7.05mm
Number of columns	1
Gutter width	N/A
Extras	Baseline grid, 24pt; 460 horizontal rows, 1.4mm apart

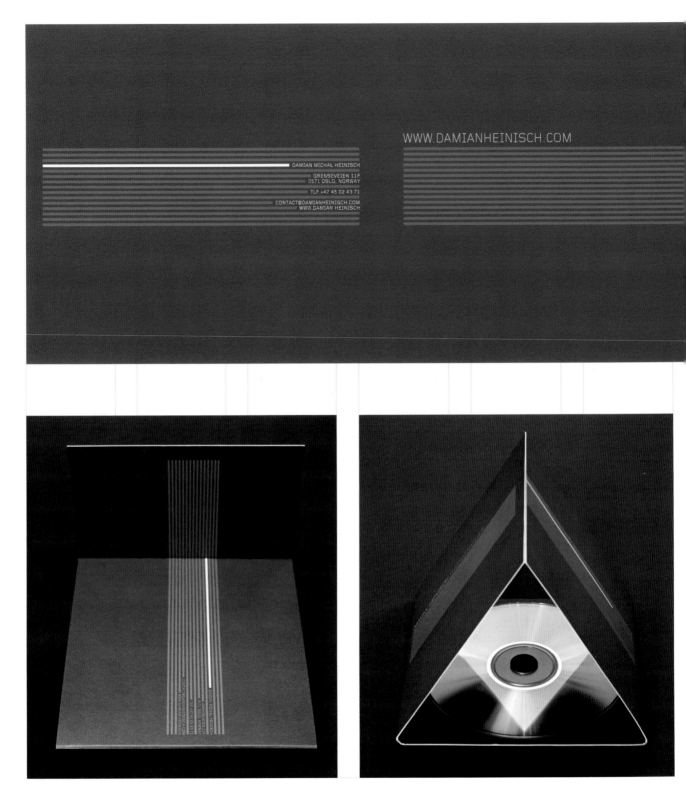

WWW.DAMIANHEINISCH.COM

DAMIAN MICHAŁ HEINISCH

GRENSEVEIEN 11F
0571 OSLO, NORWAY

TLF +47 45 02 43 71

CONTACT@DAMIANHEINISCH.COM
WWW.DAMIAN HEINISCH

DAMIAN HEINISCH\PHOTOGRAPHER

GRID SPECIFICATIONS

Page size (trimmed)	404 x 130mm
Top margin	N/A
Bottom margin	N/A
Outside margin	6.5mm
Inside margin	6.5mm
Number of columns	1
Gutter width	N/A
Extras	30 horizontal rows, 1mm apart

WWW.DAMIANHEINISCH.COM

DAMIAN HEINISCH\PHOTOGRAPHER

DAMIAN HEINISCH\PHOTOGRAPHER

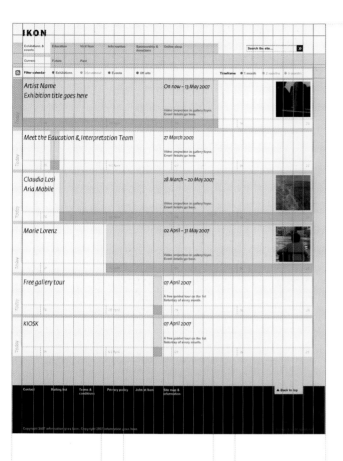

IKON GALLERY WEBSITE

Design: Dom Murphy at TAK!

Although the unit of measurement is different, grids are as relevant to web design as they are to print. The grid for this redesign of the Ikon Gallery website is based around its events calendar and monthly overview. The page is divided into 30-pixel units. This grid determines the position of all elements of the design, from navigation to the placement of information. The grid is most apparent on the events page where the area on the left represents "today," and each block represents a subsequent day. The blue/green panels show the time frame of events over the coming month, and therefore change each day.

GRID SPECIFICATIONS

Page size (trimmed)	270.933 x 361.244mm
Top margin	10.583mm
Bottom margin	10.583mm
Outside margin	10.583mm
Inside margin	10.583mm
Number of columns	15
Gutter width	8.5mm
Extras	4 horizontal fields

Magazines, newspapers & newsletters

fIK.6

Zak Kyes
Special Report
Photography
Profile
Zak Kyes
July 2007 58

152

DON'T
PANIC

01st Park Life
Take it from us, there's no better way to spend a sunny Yorkshire day than picnicking in the county's idyllic Sculpture Park. And this month you can do so with the added lure of a new series of exhibitions courtesy of the Arts Council. Between now and January, Catch This will showcase the work of four UK-based artists all characterised by their use of new media and technology. Head down this summer to enjoy new film works by Hayley Newman and Mark Lewis, and don't forget to pack the Factor Twenty. Find out more at www.ysp.co.uk.

PRINT RUN
FOR CHARITY
NO. 1048854

design
makes me sick
design
makes me better
design
makes me
complete.

PRINT RUN:
10/05/07
PRIVATE:
07/06/07
DISPLAY:

08th Picture of Health
Does design make you sick? Or, perhaps, is it the only thing worth getting up for in the morning? See how a selection of the world's top designers and studios responded to the conundrum of design's health-giving properties thanks to a new poster exhibition at London's Kemistry Gallery this month. Print Run will feature twenty A1 screenprinted creations from the likes of Experimental Jetset, Spin and North—and what's more, all entries will be on sale, with proceeds going to the Roy Castle Lung Cancer Foundation. Healthy consciences all round. Check out www.print-run.org for further information.

15th Pen and Caper
For those of you who missed it the first time round, Felt-Tip is back, and this time it's brandishing a passport. Grafik's own exhibition of hand-penned posters (courtesy of thirty top designers including Alan Fletcher and Frauke Stegman) will land this month at Cape Town's What If the World gallery. Celebrating the simple charms of felt pen on paper, not to mention the power of the imagination, Felt-Tip opens on 15 June... Next stop Namibia. Go to www.whatiftheworld.com for the lowdown.

15th Great Expectations
It's been quite some time since the legendary Great Exhibition of 1851. This summer, however, prepare to be transported back in time as the Royal College of Art stages its own version to celebrate 160 years at its current South Kensington location. Bringing together all of its graduate shows for the very first time, the RCA will erect an enormous tent in Kensington Gardens alongside a simultaneous exhibition at the College Galleries. With the work of over 400 students on display, they'll certainly be giving Prince Albert a run for his money. Full details are available at www.rca.ac.uk.

GRID SPECIFICATIONS

Page size (trimmed)	225 x 311mm
Top margin	7mm
Bottom margin	11mm
Outside margin	11mm
Inside margin	20mm
Number of columns	12
Gutter width	2.5mm
Extras	N/A

GRAFIK
Design: SEA

Designing for your peers always brings added pressures. *Grafik*'s readership had been predominantly student based, but SEA's brief was to redesign the magazine to appeal to a broader demographic. Its solution rationalized the existing design, retaining its energy within a functional and accessible structure. Developing a flexible grid was the key to this. The grid is multicolumn and also divides the page into a series of small horizontal fields. This structure supports various typographic devices—large indents and staggered text, along with continuous text, captions, standfirsts, and titling—and full-bleed, squared-up, and cut-out images.

Joachim Schmid
The Photographers'
Gallery, London
Until 17 June
By Angharad Lewis

Six Books

CAMOUFLAGE

FURNISH

100 years of Fashion Illustration

OPTIC NERVE

Mies van der Rohe

OR CITY

Insight

Always reaching for the same paper sample? Then maybe it's time to try something new. We asked the paper experts to give us the lowdown on their hottest new products, and this is what they came up with.

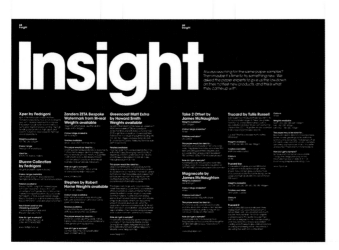

Xper by Fedrigoni

Stucco Collection by Fedrigoni

Zanders ZETA Bespoke Watermark from M-real Weights available

Stephen by Robert Horne Weights available

Greencoat Matt Extra by Howard Smith Weights available

Take 2 Offset by James McNaughton

Magnecote by James McNaughton

Trucard by Tullis Russell

PETER SAVILLE
FAC1—MCR

THURSDAY 30 NOVEMBER
6.30 LECTURE HALL

FAC1—MCR
Lecture poster designed by
AA Print Studio

Peter Saville is a designer whose practice spans the fields of graphics, creative direction and art. Past clients have included Yohji Yamamoto, Christian Dior, Givenchy, and the Whitechapel Gallery.

I invited him to speak at the AA, a place that he hadn't visited for around 20 years, but he told me he hated preparing lectures. This isn't surprising. Saville's resumé is both extensive and complex, a testament to his creative restlessness and dogged desire for ultimate independence. So I struck a deal with him. I offered to put together an image-trawl through three decades of his work, the exact results of which he wasn't to find out until the conversation began that November evening.

My reasons to get Saville to talk at the AA were twofold. On the one hand, for a certain generation (often in their 30s and 40s) Saville's sumptuous visualisations were synonymous with the best of British pop culture: Joy Division, New Order, Factory Records to name a few. Beyond the nostalgia, though, Saville continues to inspire through his inimitable capacity to disown his status as a 'graphic designer' (a label he finds limiting) while being one of the most famous graphic designers living today. It's one of the reasons Manchester awarded him the job of 'art directing' its future cultural image. Here are a few highlights from our conversation.

Shumon Basar, AACP Director

THERE IS AN EXPECTA... OF MANCHESTER

On being a graphic designer: 'I became a mercenary, a hired killer. I tried to work for clients who I didn't think were too bad. You have to work, to earn money and you just have to find a way to cope with that.'

On Joy Division's Unknown Pleasures: 'I hated the idea of things looking like record covers. If you put the name of the group on the front and put the title on the front it looks like a record cover. I did what I could with the elements – Joy Division gave me the wave pattern – but I didn't know anything, I had just left college...I wasn't even sure how you prepared artwork for print. I could only trust black and white....'

On New Order: 'The most enthusiastic reaction I got to any of the covers was "They don't much mind it." The worst was for Low-Life. When they saw it they all said, in unison, "You fucking bastard". Regret they liked because it was glossy and sexy ... Bernard said, "We might fucking sell something with this one, Peter. How long has it taken?" But they never asked me about any of them, they weren't interested.'

On Yohji Yamamoto's 1991 menswear collection: 'He said, "I don't want to see the clothes. I don't want models." In other words, "I am sick of this ... It doesn't make sense anymore." So I made a campaign that said as much. The company panicked, "This is financial suicide. We have to stop Peter, we have to stop Yohji, we have to stop it!".'

On Adidas limited edition Adicolor trainers: 'Adidas told me "Do what you want" but all of these brand partnerships are a lie... The brief made the truth plain to see, dictating the meaning of the word green. On page 1 they say I'm a "preeminent image-maker of my generation" and on page 5 they

Peter Saville logos
Various logos used in the early years of Saville's practice

GRID SPECIFICATIONS

Page size (trimmed)	176 x 250mm
Top margin	5mm
Bottom margin	24mm
Outside margin	10mm
Inside margin	20mm
Number of columns	4
Gutter width	5mm
Extras	Baseline grid, 12pt

AARCHITECTURE

Design: Wayne Daly and Grégory Ambos at AA Print Studio
with Zak Group

AArchitecture is a "news-zine" published quarterly by the Architectural Association School of Architecture and designed by Wayne Daly and Grégory Ambos. The content is broad and designed to encourage debate. Sometimes spreads show a book-within-a-book, sometimes texts are indented and staggered, sometimes full-bleed color pages are used as part of the navigation. This playful layering of information reflects the purpose of the publication—to provide a discursive forum for students, tutors, and professionals to scrutinize and shape their subject. The four-column text grid appears to be only one of the publication's defining structures.

CRISTIANO TORALDO DI FRANCIA
SUPERSTUDIO

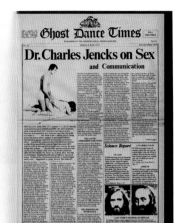

Ghost Dance Times

Dr. Charles Jencks on Sex
and Communication

---

mance goals, fosters innovation in construction.[6] Yet the role of architectural design within this context remains open to question. The latest update of the building regulations made performance evaluation more complex by introducing plant and equipment into the building's 'system performance'. This could potentially lead to environmental design principles being abandoned and the responsibility for 'making it work' being handed over to the building services engineer. Architecture could lose or give up its responsibility to perform if we no longer have environmental achievement 'per form' but only 'per system'.

An example of this scenario is apparent in the Thames Gateway, one of the UK's most celebrated 'sustainable' developments. Here architecture was used as a starting point, but the results disappointed the ambitious developer. The at times restrictive and limiting architectural features did not prove as effective at reducing carbon emissions as other on-site initiatives, such as those designed to reduce car usage. The developer has now changed approach, and in more recent projects has concentrated on embedded efficiency and low and zero carbon technologies (LZC), in physical as well as service infrastructures, to facilitate sustainable lifestyles.

Dialogue
The above examples demonstrate that many interpretations of environment and environmental performance are possible. The research cluster's ambition is to harness each group's engagement, knowledge and enthusiasm for research into EES design. In order not to be biased, the curators set out to develop a methodology that would identify research topics that address issues of interest to the design community but are also of scientific relevance. This ensures the interpretation of 'environment' matches the scale against which its performance is measured.

Cluster Activity
To gain an overview of current EES design activity the cluster organised an open competition. No specific subjects or categories were defined by the organising committee. The submissions document a self-assessment of our profession's ability to respond to environmental, ecological and sustainability-related challenges. Of particular interest are the definitions of 'environment' and 'environmental performance' of the individual entries.

The outcome of the competition and accompanying survey resulted in an exhibition preview hosted at the Architectural Association from 8 to 11 November 2006. The validity and importance of differing strands was examined during the event and recommendations were made for future research activities. The winning and shortlisted entries were exhibited, and a book is forthcoming.

During the academic year the EES Research Cluster also facilitated open and informal roundtable discussions with participants from all realms of the built environment. The aim was to communicate the different stakeholders' views on performance-related issues to EES. Participants ranged from investors and developers, architects and engineers, planners and government officials to scientists, educators and students of all levels. The complexity of addressing multiple, often contradictory demands of performance was highlighted by the contrasting views.

Conclusion
The work of the EES Research Cluster has so far revealed that the terms 'environment' and 'performance' are used vaguely and are not defined rigorously enough to evaluate design performance. The survey information taken from the submissions to the Call for Projects awaits further investigation.

The intentions of the research cluster have been presented along with the methodology employed. Gathering and identifying these relevant research strands has been the main subject of the cluster's work to date, and it is hoped that this study will stimulate an ongoing discussion involving a wide audience that stretches beyond the educational setting and the architectural profession.

Acknowledgements
The authors would like to thank Brett Steele for his encouragement and the idea of creating the research clusters at the AA. The contributions of all discussion members, judges and participants are duly acknowledged.

This text is adapted from a paper published in 'PLEA Conference Proceedings 2006', the publication accompanying the 23rd Conference on Passive and Low Energy Architecture, Geneva, Switzerland, September 2006.

Werner Gaiser is a course tutor on the Sustainable Environmental Design MA programme and a Curator of the EES Research Cluster.
Steve Hardy is Unit Master of Diploma 16 and a Curator of the EES Research Cluster.

BOB MAXWELL'S LAST LECTURE

On Wednesday 22 November, an evening event was held to mark the decision of Bob Maxwell to give up his teaching on the Histories and Theories MA programme. He marked the occasion with a lecture entitled 'Maxwell's Last Lecture'. The lecture hall was packed with students, teachers and above all with several generations of professional colleagues and friends. He opened his lecture with a melancholy roll-call of all those who were absent by reason of death. Foremost in his mind was the figure of James Stirling. The evening was full of the memory of friends.

The lecture itself must have surprised some of his audience, who perhaps were expecting a more purely architectural topic. But the teacher in him was still passionately concerned with educating his fellow architects by introducing aspects of the human sciences which could illuminate architecture, and which could provide architects with an understanding of how all objects present meaning. Most of the lecture was devoted to an outline of subjects as it was understood by de Saussure and Roland Barthes. The concerns reflected on Bob's teaching, both while he had been Dean at Princeton University and in his teaching at the AA in the last two decades.

After the lecture tributes were paid to Bob by Ed Jones and Rick Mather, who spoke warmly of Bob as an architect and a friend. From his lecture the audience were again made aware of the striking force of his complex character in which the twin aspects of Ulster Protestantism and Francophile Hedonism were intertwined. Above all the audience was aware of his underlying humanity, which has always shaped his students' experience of him.

By Mark Cousins, Director of Histories and Theories programme.

Bob Maxwell
Places were reserved long in advance for Bob Maxwell's last lecture.

Grids: Creative Solutions for Graphic Designers

Sex and

SATELLITE is an ad-hoc magazine, colonising the architecture of other AA publications, in this case AArchitecture No. 3, to create an autonomous space for editorial and curatorial projects.

There are no limitations, but possible subjects may include: student work, fictions, satrical reviews, essays, independent projects…

The idea behind this selection of Second and Third Year projects is to show some of the diversity of student work created here at the weird and remarkable Architectural Association. I am myself part of the Intermediate School; every day I see and hear about my fellow students' projects, and the richness and the creativity of the work never cease to amaze me. Everyone brings ideas and emotions into the school, producing the recipe for this glowing soup we all swim in. This is a taster – a small sample of the AA's collective creativity – that I hope you will enjoy.
– FH

Satellite 1
Guest-edited by Fredrik Hellberg
Hosted by AArchitecture Issue 3
Published by the Architectural Association
Designed by Wayne Doly/Zak Kyes

To guest-edit please write to:
contribute@aaschool.ac.uk

AZRI SYAZWAN – INTER ONE
The vitrine is required to hold and unfold information about a specific product. In this case a football was the subject of interest. While the first layer of the vitrine communicates the history of developing the 'modern' football, the next layer reveals the true nature of football production, including its darker side and the nature of the construction itself. The user deconstructs the components of the football on the wired vitrine placed onto specified areas on the board, and in the process reveals video information through a computer and projector located elsewhere.

I DO NOT WANT TO TALK TO YOU ABOUT ARCHITECTURE. I DETEST TALK ABOUT ARCHITECTURE.

LE CORBUSIER, AA AFTER-DINNER SPEECH, 1 APRIL 1953

AArchitecture   Issue 4   Summer   2007   1

VERSO

AArchitecture
News from the Architectural Association
Issue 4 / Summer 2007
aaschool.net

©2007
All rights reserved.
Published by Architectural Association,
36 Bedford Square, London WC1B 3ES.

Contact:
contribute@aaschool.ac.uk
Nicola Quinn +44 (0) 207 887 4000

To send news briefs:
news@aaschool.ac.uk

EDITORIAL TEAM
Brett Steele, Editorial Director
Nicola Quinn, Managing Editor
Zak Kyes / Zak Group, Art Director
Wayne Daly, Graphic Designer
Alex Lorente
Fredrik Hellberg

ACKNOWLEDGEMENTS
Valerie Bennett
Pamela Johnston
Marilyn Sparrow
Hinda Sklar
Russell Bestley

Printed by Cassochrome, Belgium

CONTRIBUTORS

Rosa Ainley
<eventslist@aaschool.ac.uk>

Edward Bottoms
<edward@aaschool.ac.uk>

Mark Cousins
<markcousins@aaschool.ac.uk>

Wayne Daly
<daly_wa@aaschool.ac.uk>

Margaret Dewhurst
<margiedewhurst@hotmail.com>

Zak Kyes
<z@zak.to>

Aram Mooradian
<aram.mooradian@gmail.com>

Harmony Murphy
<harmonymurphy@gmail.com>

Joel Newman
<joel@aaschool.ac.uk>

Kitty O'Grady
<ogrady_ki@aaschool.ac.uk>

Mark Prizeman

Simone Sagi
<simone@aaschool.ac.uk>

Vasilis Stroumpakos
<vasi@00110.org>

COVER

Front Cover:
Le Corbusier, AA after-dinner speech
1 April 1953

Front inner cover: Hans Scharoun's
Staatsbibliothek
Back inner cover: Peter Eisenman's
Memorial to the Murdered Jews of Europe
Photos: Timothy Deal, on AA Members'
trip to Berlin, 19–22 April 2007

* * * *

PEIGNOT

MARY TYLER MOORE
edited by
MARY TYLER MOORE

Headlines in the issue are set in Peignot,
a geometrically constructed sans-serif
display typeface designed by A. M.
Cassandre in 1937. It was commissioned
by the French foundry Peignot et Deberny.
The typeface is notable for not having
a traditional lower-case, but in its place
a 'multi-case' combining traditional
lower-case and small capital characters.
The typeface achieved some popularity
in poster and advertising publishing from
its release through the late 1940s. Use of
Peignot declined with the growth of the
International Typographic Style which
favoured less decorative, more objective
typeface. Peignot experienced a revival
in the 1970s as the typeface used on *The
Mary Tyler Moore Show*. While often
classified as 'decorative', the face is a
serious exploration of typographic form
and legibility.
Taken from:
http://en.wikipedia.org/wiki/Peignot

Body text is set in Sabon Bold.

Architectural Association (Inc.),
Registered Charity No. 311083. Company
limited by guarantee. Registered in
England No. 171402. Registered office
as above.

AArchitecture

WE DO NOT KNOW EACH OTHER BUT WE READ EACH
OTHER AS SIGNS, WE BUILD UP A CODE OF
RECOGNITION THAT ENABLES US TO IDENTIFY PEOPLE
AND OBJECTS THROUGH THEIR ATTRIBUTES. MARK COUSINS PG 27

THE BUILDING SITE IS
THE IDEAL PLACE
TO SHARE DESIRES
AND KNOWLEDGE
AND BUILD A RELEVANT
VISION FOR THE
FUTURE, IN THE INTEREST
OF EVERYONE

SATELLITE 2

GUEST-EDITED BY
AA FOUNDATION UNIT STAFF
AND STUDENTS

HOLLYWOOD TOWER

A FILM BY RENÉ DAALDER & REM KOOLHAAS

Photography by Pete Moss

SIMON ESTERSON: You are one of the very few type designers to have worked with metal type-setting, then photosetting, through the digital revolution, and then on to screen-based, non-print media. How do you feel about what has happened to typeface design in the last 25 years?

MATTHEW CARTER: (laughs) It's been 50 years, by the way, since I left school and started working in type. I'm happy to have had a traditional training, although even by the late 1950s making type by hand was obsolete commercially speaking. It never really had a commercial application for me. It's been very interesting to live through these various changes in technology. Though most of type's history, sons, grandsons, great grandsons came and went and the technology never changed. The opposite has been true in the last 50 years: the technology has changed faster than the typefaces if anything. So it's been interesting.

My own feeling about it: if you look at all the things that go into making a typeface, and you gave them a score out of ten, I would say that the technical part of it is worth one or two on that scale. In other words, however the type is made, about at least 80 per cent of it is still the same, whatever tools you use. There are exceptions to that. When I worked on Bell Centennial for the United States phonebooks, where the environment it's used in is rather hostile, the technology played a larger part. For phone books, we're talking about six point type on newsprint. When I did the screen fonts for Microsoft, I think more than 20 percent of that was technical influence. So that's my feeling about it. A lot of people disagree and believe that type cut in steel has different qualities, and I can look at beautiful letterpress printing from metal type and I can see that things have been lost. But in my opinion the gains in digital type far outweigh the losses.

It's a fatuous thing to say in a way, but if I had my choice of period in which to have worked in this business I would choose exactly the one that I happen to have lucked into, precisely because of all these changes. I'm endlessly glad to have survived into the digital era because I regard that as the best technology we've ever had. There are some drawbacks, there have been some losses, but for me, it's just a dream.

SE: I suppose designers who are used to working on a Mac, take being able to track and hem type for granted, when actually tracking and kerning with metal type-setting was very difficult, if not sometimes impossible.

MC: Kerning is a good example: strictly speaking, there was kerning in the latter days of film composition, there were some refinement programmes and so on, but essentially it became part of type with the coming of Type 1 PostScript fonts, True Type and so on. I regard kerning tables as a great blessing for typography.

MC: Once, the making of type was almost like a secret society; there was the mystique of being a punch-cutter and type-maker. Then it became quite an industrial process and Monotype and Linotype seemed to rule the world in composition terms: if they didn't make a typeface then it wasn't going to be made. Now, there's this incredible blossoming, where it seems as if everybody can be a type designer if they want to.

MC: I'm entirely happy about that. I'm sometimes a bit nostalgic about the time when it was a tiny club, when you had to go through painful initiations in order to be a type designer, but on balance, I'm glad the whole thing got blown wide open by the computer and particularly the coming of open font formats in the late 80s. There was a huge flow of interest in type design and it got democratised. There was no longer just a priesthood, but a sort of laity as well. I think a huge amount of very interesting work was done then, and some continues. What there is much more of, of course, are people who are primarily graphic designers or typographers, who occasionally make a typeface as a labour of love. This would have never happened in the old regime because it was just too hard to get started. Now, it's not uncommon to see student portfolios with typefaces they've designed and I'm completely delighted by that. It doesn't mean to say that everything made under these conditions are things that I like, but cream rises, and out of that ferment come very good things.

SE: Type design is quite stratified – even in the Victorian era you had display type and text type, and there's been a lot of activity in recent years in exuberant display typography. While you do some of these things too, a lot of your work is about what I'd call

industrial-strength text typesetting.

MC: Yes, I think in my case there isn't a moral issue there, it's just a matter of temperament. Because I made my start in type founding, I never went to design school, I think that I've always been interested in these rather 'thorny, problem-solving projects, which are largely text faces. I have done a few display faces as well, but I seem to have mostly been asked to work in the text field, and I'm very happy with that. I don't think you're ever going to be a type designer unless you accept that you have to work within certain constraints.

SE: How does it work? Do you sit at home and wait for the phone to ring, with somebody saying 'we've got a problem,' or do you wake up in the morning thinking 'I have this beautiful idea for a lower case A, now I just need to do the rest of the alphabet?'

MC: I suppose both things happen. In an ideal world, life would be a nice balance between speculative projects and commissions. In fact I'm not good at bright ideas. If you sat me down in front of a blank computer screen on a Monday it would still be blank on the Friday. But if you said to me 'we have this typeface and it's a bit too heavy and too wide, fix it up,' I'd have something for you.

I tend not to get butts from the blue very often although for example, a typeface like Mantinia was the direct result of going into an exhibition at the Royal Academy in 1992 and looking at some lettering there. I wish that happened more often, I wish I could say 'I'm going down the road now, I'm going to see a piece of vernacular lettering which is going to turn me on and become a wonderful typeface,' it doesn't normally happen.

SE: So it's not the case that you walk down the street and see so much inspiring typography...

MC: Obviously, I do see things I like, walking down the street, looking at books and so on. A good proportion of the faces that I've done have been based, to some degree, on historical models, and I'm interested in the history of typeface design, but, as you say, a lot of my faces do come about because somebody calls me up with a particular problem.

Type designer Matthew Carter (facing page) was born in England in the 1930s. He trained as a punch cutter in the Netherlands before working as a typography consultant for Crosfield electronics. He later worked for Mergenthaler-Linotype in New York before becoming typography consultant to Her Majesty's Stationery Office in the 1960s. In 1981 he set up Bitstream Inc with Mike Parker in Massachusetts, the first independent American company to manufacture digital type. In 1992 he founded Carter & Cone Type Inc with Cherie Cone. Matthew Carter was named a Royal Designer for Industry in 1981. In the recent visit to London, Carter gave a talk at the Design Museum. For future events and exhibitions see www.designmuseum.org

Simon Esterson is a magazine and newspaper designer. He has been art director of The Guardian in London and creative director of Domus in Milan.

With thanks to the St Bride Printing Library

A Life in Type

(Part One)

Matthew Carter is the world's leading type designer. In the apt setting of the St Bride Printing Library, editorial designer Simon Esterson talks to him about his 50 years in the industry. Continued next month

Continued next month

"MANTINIA WAS THE DIRECT RESULT OF GOING INTO AN EXHIBITION AT THE ROYAL ACADEMY IN 1992 AND LOOKING AT SOME LETTERING THERE, I WISH THAT HAPPENED MORE OFTEN, I WISH I COULD SAY, "I'M GOING DOWN THE ROAD NOW, I'M GOING TO SEE A PIECE OF VERNACULAR LETTERING WHICH IS GOING TO TURN ME ON AND BECOME A TYPEFACE"

Sports Illustrated asked me to design them a new text face, a bit heavier than Times, but no wider, because the editors didn't want to cut down on words, and I think they were absolutely right to say that – why would they sacrifice their writing so that I can go to hell with myself and make some unsuitable typeface?

To celebrate its seventieth anniversary, Penguin has commissioned the Pocket Penguins series: 70 covers from 70 different artists, who were paid just £70 each. By Steve Hare

For a graphic designer, having your own print works to play with must be just about the ultimate toy. Issey Kitagawa makes full use of his. By Patrick Burgoyne

GRID SPECIFICATIONS

Page size (trimmed)	280 x 280mm
Top margin	8mm
Bottom margin	18mm
Outside margin	8mm
Inside margin	18mm
Number of columns	15
Gutter width	4.5mm
Extras	N/A

CREATIVE REVIEW

Design: Nathan Gale at Creative Review

When the design magazine *Creative Review* was redesigned, it gave
art director Nathan Gale an opportunity to introduce one grid that
was flexible enough to accommodate all the different material the
magazine shows. Previously it had used more than one grid, and
Gale thought this was an opportune time to rationalize the design
system. The new grid is multicolumn and divided into small
horizontal fields. By combining columns and fields, text can run
to the three different widths the magazine needs, and images
of different sizes and scales can be positioned easily and flexibly.

ABRAM GAMES MAXIMUM MEANING FROM MINIMUM MEANS

By Carmen Martínez-López

Abram Games (1914–96) was one of the great poster designers of the 20th century. His contribution to the development of graphic communication was even more remarkable for having been made within the constricts of propaganda communication during World War II. Images such as *Your Talk May Kill Your Comrades* or *Don't Crow About What You Know About* applied modern design sophistication to the primary messages of wartime in a witty and effective way. Although Games' career coincided with the demise of his original trade as a graphic artist, as the promotional power of posters diminished in the face of television and colour supplements, he remained productive throughout. Following Games' death in 1996, the illustrator David Gentleman FCSD wrote that:

"All Abram Games' designs were recognisably his own. They had vigour, imagination, passion and individuality ... And he was lucky—and clever—in contriving, over a long and creative working life, to keep on doing what he did best."

SELECTED ILLUSTRATIONS
LEFT TO RIGHT

Festival of Britain, 1951
© Estate of Abram Games

British Railways poster
to promote holidays
in Blackpool, 1952
© Estate of Abram Games

London Underground, 1937
© Transport for London

CONCERTS

BALLET

OPERA

CHORAL

RECITALS

The Designer October & November '03

NEWS & EVENTS

Lectures

Grids: Creative Solutions for Graphic Designers

GRID SPECIFICATIONS

Page size (trimmed)	297 x 210mm
Top margin	12mm
Bottom margin	21.1mm
Outside margin	10mm
Inside margin	10mm
Number of columns	6
Gutter width	5mm
Extras	Baseline grid, 11pt starting at 12mm

THE DESIGNER

Design: Brad Yendle at Design Typography

The Designer is a 32-page magazine produced every month by the Chartered Society of Designers. Given its readership, any redesign would be a tough brief, particularly as the objective was to increase appeal by injecting visual excitement. Inspired by the work of Willy Fleckhaus and Simon Esterson, designer Brad Yendle introduced a simple six-column grid. By combining columns, this could accommodate text and a variety of picture sizes. Yendle paid particular attention to typographic detailing, making sure that the choice of font, type sizes, and leading gave optimum legibility in his three-column text structure.

Grids: Creative Solutions for Graphic Designers

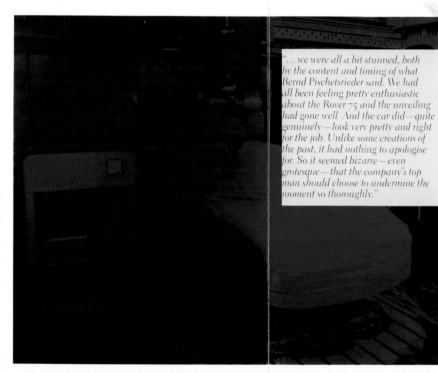

> "... we were all a bit stunned, both by the content and timing of what Bernd Pischetsrieder said. We had all been feeling pretty enthusiastic about the Rover 75 and the unveiling had gone well. And the car did—quite genuinely—look very pretty and right for the job. Unlike some creations of the past, it had nothing to apologise for. So it seemed bizarre—even grotesque—that the company's top man should choose to undermine the moment so thoroughly."

OPPOSITE

Rover's troubles and threats of difficulties in the market all stem from the car. The clear speech of a long shadow, over the entire West Midland, and the automotive design sector.

To be sure, Rover replaces in all, the linkage of the assembly process ... we were all a bit stunned. So it by the event of and timing of what Bernd Pischetsrieder said. We had all been feeling pretty enthusiastic about the Rover 75 and the unveiling had gone well. Huge crowds, lots of applause. And the car did, quite genuinely, look very pretty and right for the job. Unlike some creations of the past, it had absolutely nothing to apologise for. So it seemed bizarre, even grotesque, that the company's top man should choose to undermine the moment so thoroughly. He deliberately set in motion pressing the car the way they would naturally, have about defined the weakness when one less, became a high and industry of a degree of luxury uncertainty that could have been needed. So the newspapers and magazines were, dour of Rover seems rather than Rover's brilliant new executive car.

In fact, it would seem the reasoning behind the all-adverse speech was to get the rumour and scale force, brown undermine it, accept only leave—allow Pischetsrieder to develop Longbridge in accordance with his plans, and get the necessary production there. The nicer's royalty of the lime was Walter Hasselkus, who resigned as the Chairman and Chief Executive of Rover in the 2nd December 1998. He simply stated that he was going because of that to operations under way, although it looked like he was describing a sinking ship he did not stay away from. I now agree event, which at the time looked so though it could help save the company. Pischetsrieder certainly did not give up either—and although Rover was expected to cut over 2000 some 1500 million in such he sought to promote the further design and development of the 75 and 200.

Continuing the new Sequel were losing to keep the faith in the design of the 75 model would be difficult without an analysis given in order to benefit the financial burden on new and thankfully the trusts were making it enough to accept to secure to guarantee the future of Longbridge and the 200 model. The total sum of the 75 design and development programme would be £400 billion, of which £1.5 billion was to cover the cost of the Longbridge machine. Pischetsrieder knew that the state would be nervous about spending such a vast sum of money, and although the £45 million was related cut went some way towards approving them, there would need to be further concessions. Pischetsrieder therefore decided crafts-

CRAFTSMANSHIP

MAN

SHIP

Grids: Creative Solutions for Graphic Designers

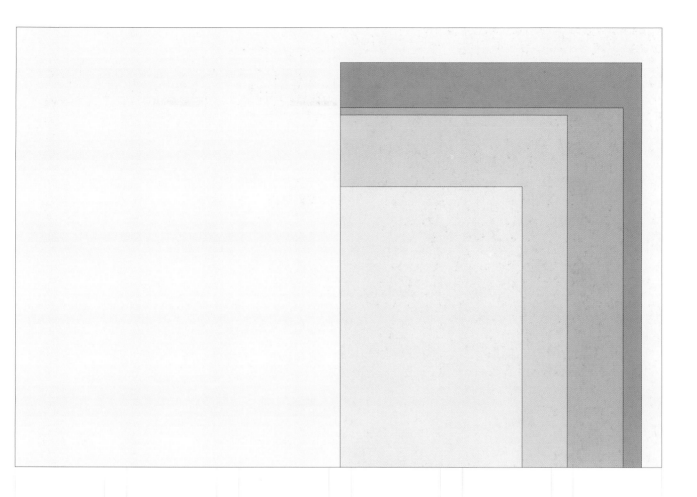

GRID SPECIFICATIONS

Page size (trimmed)	210 x 297mm
Format/Grid 1	200 x 270mm
Format/Grid 2	185 x 239mm
Format/Grid 3	146 x 234mm
Format/Grid 4	115 x 185mm
Number of columns	N/A
Gutter width	N/A
Extras	N/A

GRAY MAGAZINE

Design: Clare McNally, Lane Gry, and Risto Kalmre

GRAy is the official magazine of the Gerrit Rietveld Academy in Amsterdam. An annual publication, it is designed, edited, and produced by graduating graphic design students. The three designers, Clare McNally, Lane Gry, and Risto Kalmre, wanted GRAy to reflect its theme—craftsmanship—partly through its precision, but also through their hands-on skill in putting it together. They evolved two approaches to the grid.

The first grid was derived from the different formats of various types of publication: the novel, the art book, technical manuals, and A4 (210 x 297mm [c. 8⅛ x 11⅝in]) magazines. These four formats were amalgamated to form the underlying structure governing the placement text and images.

A test scan using the reprographic scanner.   *Each spread was laid out by hand as an "image."*

The day of scanning.

The scan of pages 2 and 3.

The second grid was generated in InDesign to give a consistent
position for folios and running feet. Each section of the magazine
was printed and cut out according to the various formats. These
spreads were then positioned by hand according to the InDesign
grid, then scanned and reprinted, making the final design process
interactive in a totally physical way.

DUMB PLANETS ARE ROUND TOO

Artist_John Isaacs

Last night I dreamt that I lived in the ocean. I felt safe with all these fish swimming around me, it never occurred to me that they would eat me. I felt that because I was not hungry that they too were not thinking about food. Even the sharks, which would normally scare me to death, seemed to pay me no interest.

Of course I wasn't really there, so it's possible that I was invisible to all these creatures. Though it was strange to be underwater, it didn't feel unnatural, I had no trouble holding my breath, and I felt incredibly relaxed watching them all move so silently and effortlessly through the water. The way we

were down there me and the fish - was very laid back.

Then it occurred to me that people don't really like one another. That they do all these terrible things to one another for reasons they themselves cannot begin to explain, and even when they love one another and truly believe this to be the case there's always something in the way. I started to understand that people are all essentially alone. Outcasts not just from nature, but one another.

In the ocean everything is what it is.

The oddest looking creature is that way for

a reason, a function, but for us it is different. With all that we have, we are beyond evolution, beyond time to the extent that each person represents their own cosmos - a species evolving from birth to extinction at death. It is consciousness, which brings us apart.

This realisation started to merge into others, I lost track, got confused, and possibly a little anxious, trying both to follow and remember my thoughts. It was as though I was witnessing an immense explosion, which contained all the components of it's origin within the fragmentary pieces flying through space. People I never knew drifted next to more

familiar faces. Everyone that ever lived, and that ever would, everything ever made and that would be invented, spread out from the center of this thought and at just the point when I was beginning to loose sight of the edges it stopped still and took on the appearance of a huge cloud. I then felt rather than saw, that everyone was connected to one another by thin nerve like threads, which became visible as I thought about them. It was impossible to tell which one came before the other or if my thought and their appearance were simultaneous. Everything was there.

I saw you in there too.

#8
24   Next Level   Next Level   #8
                                                                                               25

Façade

Grids: Creative Solutions for Graphic Designers

DUMB PLANETS ARE ROUND TOO

Artist: John Isaacs

Last night I dreamt that I lived in the ocean. I felt safe with all these fish swimming around me, it never occurred to me that they would eat me. I felt that because I was not hungry that they too were not thinking about food. Even the sharks, which would normally scare me to death, seemed to pay me no interest.

Of course I wasn't really there, so it's possible that I was invisible to all these creatures. Though it was strange to be underwater, it didn't feel unnatural. I had no trouble holding my breath, and I felt incredibly relaxed watching them all move so silently and effortlessly through the water. The way we

were down there me and the fish - was very laid back.

Then it occurred to me that people don't really like one another. That they do all these terrible things to one another for reasons they themselves cannot begin to explain, and even when they love one another and truly believe this to be the case there's always something in the way. I started to understand that people are all essentially alone. Outcasts not just from nature, but one another.

In the ocean everything is what it is.

The oddest looking creature is that way for

a reason, a function, but for us it is different. With all that we have, we are beyond evolution, beyond time to the extent that each person represents their own cosmos - a species evolving from birth to extinction at death. It is consciousness, which brings us apart.

This realisation started to merge into others, I lost track, got confused, and possibly a little anxious, trying both to follow and remember my thoughts. It was as though I was witnessing an immense explosion, which contained all the components of it's origin within the fragmentary pieces flying through space. People I never knew drifted next to more

familiar faces. Everyone that ever lived, and that ever would, everything ever made and that would be invented, spread out from the center of this thought and at just the point when I was beginning to loose sight of the edges it stopped still and took on the appearance of a huge cloud. I then felt rather than saw, that everyone was connected to one another by thin nerve like threads, which became visible as I thought about them. It was impossible to tell which one came before the other or if my thought and their appearance were simultaneous. Everything was there.

GRID SPECIFICATIONS

Page size (trimmed)	235 x 304mm
Top margin	7mm
Bottom margin	20mm
Outside margin	7mm
Inside margin	15mm
Number of columns	5
Gutter width	7mm
Extras	Baseline grid, 6mm

NEXT LEVEL: STORYTELLERS

Design: Julian Harriman-Dickinson at Harriman Steel

Each issue of *Next Level*, a biannual photography, arts, and ideas magazine, is based on a different theme, and the design reflects this. From font usage to grid systems, each issue is designed from scratch. The theme of this issue was film. The color palette is derived from TV color bands and designer Julian Harriman-Dickinson introduced test cards as novel graphic devices. He wanted his design to be "so clear and transparent that my mum could see how it was done," so he deliberately foregrounded the five-column grid.

On Par

PHotoEspaña, now in its 8th year, took place from 1st June to the 17th July across 50 galleries in Madrid and showed the work of nearly 100 international photographers. It was a group portrait of La Cuidad/The City, exploring the parameters of 21st Century city living and a variety of issues were brought to the fore: What are the visions of utopia and dystopia? What are the changing relationships between public and private spheres, the centre and the periphery? What are the consequences of post industrial economies on the urban fabric? How have urban policies altered the experience of the city? What are the domestic preoccupations of the way we live today?

TAKE CARE OF YOUR SCARF TATJANA

Grids: Creative Solutions for Graphic Designers

Q: Do you prefer television, movies on a big screen, or surfing the Internet?

I have a completely schizophrenic relationship with television. When I'm feeling lonely, I adore it, particularly since there's been cable. It's curious how cable offers an entire catalog of antidotes to the poisons of standard TV. If one network shows a ridiculous TV movie about Napoleon, you can flip over to the History Channel to hear Henri Guillemin's brilliantly mean commentary on it. If a literary program makes us submit to a parade of currently fashionable female monsters, we can change over to Mezzo to contemplate the luminous face of Hélène Grimaud surrounded by her wolves, and it's as if the others never existed. Now there are moments when I remember I am not alone, and that's when I fall apart. The exponential growth of stupidity and vulgarity is something that everyone has noticed, but it's not just a vague sense of disgust - it's a concrete quantifiable fact (you can measure it by the volume of the cheers that greet the talk-show hosts, which have grown by an alarming number of decibels in the last five years) and a crime against humanity. Not to mention the permanent aggressions against the French language. . . . And since you are exploiting my Russian penchant for confession, I must say the worst: I am allergic to commercials. In the early Sixties, making commercials was perfectly acceptable; now, it's something that no one will own up to. I can do nothing about it. This manner of placing the mechanism of the lie in the service of praise has always irritated me, even if I have to admit that this diabolical patron has occasionally given us some of the most beautiful images you can see on the small screen (have you seen the David Lynch commercial with the blue lips?). But cynics always betray themselves, and there is a small consolation in the industry's own terminology: they stop short of calling themselves so they call themselves creatives.

And the movies in all this?

For the reasons mentioned above, and under the orders of Jean-Luc, I've said for a long time that films should be seen first in theaters, and that television and video are only there to refresh your memory. Now that I no longer have any time at all to go to the cinema, I've started seeing films by lowering my eyes, with an ever increasing sense of sinfulness (this interview is indeed becoming Dostoevskian). But to tell the truth I no longer watch many films, only those by friends, or curiosities that an American acquaintance tapes for me on TCM. There is too much to see on the news, on the music channels or on the indispensable Animal Channel. And I feed my hunger for fiction with what is by far the most accomplished source: those great American TV series, like The Practice. There is a knowledge in them, a sense of story and economy, of ellipsis, a science of framing and of cutting, a dramaturgy and an acting style that has no equal anywhere, and certainly not in Hollywood.

Q: La Jetée inspired a video by David Bowie and a film by Terry Gilliam. And there's also a bar called 'La Jetée' in Japan. How do you feel about this cult? Does Terry Gilliam's imagination interact with yours?

Terry's imagination is rich enough that there's no need to play with comparisons. Certainly, for me 12 Monkeys is a magnificent film (there are people who think they are flattering me by saying otherwise, that La Jetée is much better - the world is a strange place). It's just one of the happy signs, like Bowie's video, like the bar in Shinjuku (Hello, Tomoyo! To know that for almost 40 years, a group of Japanese are getting slightly drunk beneath my images every night - that's worth more to me than any number of Oscars!), that have accompanied the strange destiny of this particular film. It was made like a piece of automatic writing. I was filming Le Joli mai, completely immersed in the reality of Paris 1962, and the euphoric discovery of direct cinema (you will never make me say 'cinema vérité') and on the crew's day off, I photographed a story I didn't completely understand. It was in the editing that the pieces of the puzzle came together, and it wasn't me who designed the puzzle. I'd have a hard time taking credit for it. It just happened, that's all.

Q: You are a witness of history. Are you still interested in world affairs? What makes you jump to your feet, react, shout?

Right now there are some very obvious reasons to jump, and we know them all so well that I have very little desire to talk more about them. What remains are the small, personal resentments. For me, 2002 will be the year of a failure that I have never had the chance to talk about. It begins with a flashback, as in The Barefoot Contessa. Among our circle in the Forties, the one we all considered to be a future great writer was François Vernet. He had already published three books, and the fourth was to be a collection of short stories that he had written during the Occupation, with a vigor and an insolence that obviously left him little hope with the censors. The book wasn't published until 1945. Meanwhile, François had died in Dachau. I don't mean to label him as a martyr - that's not my style. Even if this death puts a kind of symbolic seal on a destiny that was already quite singular, the texts themselves are of such a rare quality that there is no need for reasons other than literary in order to love them and introduce them to others. François Maspero wasn't wrong when he said in an article that they "transverse time with only an extreme lightness of being as ballast." Because last year a courageous publisher, Michel Reynaud (Tiresias), fell in love with the book and took the risk of reprinting it. I did everything I could to mobilize people I knew, not in order to make it the event of the season but simply to get it talked about. But no, there were too many books during that season. Except for Maspero, there wasn't a word in the press. And so - failure.

Q: Was that reaction too personal?

By chance, it was paired with a similar event, to which no line of friendship attached me. The same year, Capriccio Records released a new recording by Viktor Ullman. Under his name alone, this time. Previously, he and Gideon Klein had been recorded as Theresienstadt composers (for younger readers: Theresienstadt was the model concentration camp designed to be visited by the Red Cross, the Nazis made a film about it called The Führer Gives a City to the Jews.) With the best intentions in the world, [calling them] that was a way of putting them both back in the camp. If Messiaen had died after he composed the 'Quartet for the End of Time', would he be the prison camp composer?

This record is astounding: it contains lieder based on texts by Hölderlin and Rilke, and one is struck by the vertiginous thought that, at that particular time, no one was glorifying the true German culture more than this Jewish musician who was soon to die at Auschwitz. This time, there wasn't total silence - just a few flattering lines on the arts pages. Wasn't it worth a bit more? What makes me mad isn't that what we call "media coverage" is generally reserved for people I personally find rather mediocre - that's a matter of opinion and I wish them no ill. It's that the noise, in the electronic sense, just gets louder and louder and ends up drowning out everything, until it becomes a monopoly just like the way supermarkets force out the corner stores. That the unknown writer and the brilliant musician have the right to the same consideration as the corner store keeper may be too much to ask. And as long as you've handed me the microphone, I would add one more name to my list of the little injustices of the year: no one has said enough of the most beautiful book I have read for a long time, short stories again - La Fiancée d'Odessa, by [filmmaker] Edgardo Cozarinsky.

Q: Have your travels made you suspicious of dogmatism?

I think I was already suspicious when I was born. I must have traveled a lot before then!

Sample this highlight honest: Salute adieu for the Paris days. Liberation. Originally published in Liberation, March 3, 2003. With thanks to Jérôme de Baecque.

© 2003 by Special Passalde and Annick Peigné

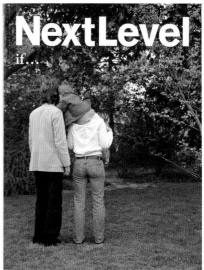

GRID SPECIFICATIONS

Page size (trimmed)	235 x 304mm
Top margin	9mm
Bottom margin	30mm
Outside margin	9mm
Inside margin	15mm
Number of columns	5
Gutter width	7mm
Extras	N/A

NEXT LEVEL: IF...

Design: Nick Steel at Harriman Steel

Next Level, a themed photography, arts, and ideas magazine, is produced twice a year. Each theme calls for a different design. This issue was inspired by the idea of simplification. Designer Nick Steel wanted the publication to be visually naive. He introduced larger-than-standard type for the body copy, and alternates between very simple two- and three-column grids. Space is introduced where possible, and images are generally squared up as determined by the grid.

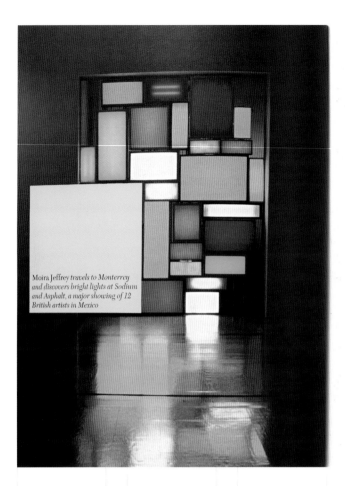

Moira Jeffrey travels to Monterrey and discovers bright lights at Sodium and Asphalt, a major showing of 12 British artists in Mexico

MAP
You are here. Journeys in Contemporary Art

FRANCIS ALŸS / NATHAN COLEY /
SIMON STARLING / GRAHAM
FAGEN / BEAGLES AND RAMSAY /
JERUSALEM / MEXICO / ARGYLL

Issue 1 / Spring 2005
£4.95

The new international art magazine from Scotland

Certain of NOTHING:

Grids: Creative Solutions for Graphic Designers

GRID SPECIFICATIONS

Page size (trimmed)	221 x 277mm
Top margin	10mm
Bottom margin	20mm
Outside margin	10mm
Inside margin	18mm
Number of columns	12
Gutter width	3mm
Extras	Baseline grid, 10.5pt

MAP MAGAZINE
Design: Matt Willey and Zoë Bather

MAP is an international art magazine published in Scotland. From the outset, designers Matt Willey and Zoë Bather felt a duty to display the work in a visually arresting, yet respectful and clear way. Willey and Bather took the rich, but functional language of cartography as their visual starting point. The grid on the cover divides the space so that the masthead can occupy any of six possible positions, depending upon its relationship to the image behind. The same grid determines the position of the standfirsts that announce each article. The grid on the review pages is plotted using cross-marks that borrow from the language of maps, while the navigation system uses blue vertical lines positioned next to the folios like lines of longitude.

GLASGOW
LONDON
PARIS
WASHI
NBU

REVIEW

AND MULL

Still, all is well, because we are each given the beautifully designed catalogue of Morrison's most recent show, and the paintings of slate quarries and cottages in the Easdale area, with the sea and islands looming, do make a positive impact. Apparently, Jolomo has had a couple of exhibitions organised by Kranenburg and Fowler on the Caledonian MacBrayne ferry. But there is no such luck for us, and our boat to Mull does not even have 'WE ARE NOT AFRAID OF THE INNER HEBRIDES' emblazoned along its flank. Nevertheless, we travel across the water in good spirits, with me wearing a brand new Oban-bought t-shirt that sports the slogan 'BOOTY FUN CLUB'. We give Mull a good going over. At least we

drive backwards and forwards along the coastal road that surrounds the great lump of a place. Our jaunt culminates in a visit to the arts centre, An Tobar ('Gaelic for the well'), in the island's capital of Tobermory. Again it's lottery funding that's responsible for the building itself, which contains studio space for both artists and musicians, a café and a gallery. And again, a shortage of revenue funding leaves the gallery scrabbling to make the most of its potential. The island's population is only 2,500, so perhaps it's not surprising that Lee Hendrick – the person we first met this morning in her Workshop Gallery nearby, whose prominent piece we came across on the island's sculpture trail, and who is responsible for the set design for the production of Jekyll and Hyde we will be seeing this evening – is here to greet us in her role as An Tobar's visual arts officer. One head, myriad hats. Isn't that how it goes in the film *Local Hero*?

Anyway, she introduces us to the gallery installation 'Passing', by Ursula Ziegler. This is a straight transfer of the artist's 2004 degree show from Glasgow School of Art. Every day for a month, Ziegler pushed a wheelbarrow through a circular route in the city centre, the flat-tyred, rusty old vehicle supporting a pane of glass in which the artist watched the world pass by upside down. The perversity, delicacy and tenacity of her viewing experience are captured in the photographs and slides that make up the uncompromising installation. German-born Ziegler, formerly a resident of Mull, was artist-in-residence at An Tobar for a month in 2004 in which period she developed further her ideas of self-consciously walking and looking by 'invigilating the land' with the use of the frame of a chair stripped of its furnishings. She both sat on the object and used it as a frame in which to regard the Mull landscape at different times of the day and in the endlessly varying weather conditions. An attempt is being made to get funding so that a future show in the gallery can bring together Ziegler's field-work for the people of the island to mull over.

When I awake on the last morning of the tour, conscious that the long drinking evenings and the early cooked breakfasts haven't been leaving much time for sleep, I feel surprisingly fresh. I pull on my second new t-shirt,

a primary blue job overprinted in red with the words 'NODDY GOES TO TOYLAND'. I switch on my mobile. Shit, there is no message from the director of Cove Park, which means I won't be bailing out of the bus journey back to Glasgow to explore Open Studios site – just outside the territory of the Highlands and Islands development agency and so not scheduled into our tour. Never mind, because on a future journey I will explore Cove Park and investigate its seven annual residencies and close links with Glasgow School of Art. Never mind also, because I still have the present day at my disposal.

On one wall of my Tobermory Hotel bedroom is a recent oil by Jolomo whose nightscape – a dramatically moonlit bay – neatly complements the view through the window. The real Tobermory Bay presents a placid sunrise, with red infusing the otherwise pale blue sky. The wash of pink above the horizon takes me back to the very thing that started me off on this journey – the pink poster advertising the Chris Johanson show at the Modern Institute. Let me recall it in detail: from the mouth of a crudely drawn figure with the letters 'CONTEMPORARY' running

through him or her, is the observation, 'Gradually systems are breaking down'. A figure with a cube-shaped head replies via a voice-bubble of its own. 'Problem does not compute'. When in Glasgow, I appreciated the concern of the despairing city dweller. But now, after ten – admittedly privileged – journeys, and from a non-urban perspective, things simply don't look the same. To me mind it's the cube-headed modernist who laments, 'Gradually systems are breaking down'. The reply from the upright organic figure, whom I see as an amalgam of Benny Nesbit, Joseph Beuys, and Ursula Ziegler, is a resoundingly confident, 'Problem does not compute'.

Duncan McLaren is an author and arts writer. He has recently contributed to Infallible: In Search of the Real George Elliot, published by ARTicle Press

www.themoderninstitute.com
www.somewhere.org.uk Nina Pope,
Karen Guthrie and their Bata-ville coach trip
www.kilmartin.org
www.blinkred.com Demarco and Beuys
www.kranenburg-fowler.com
www.antobar.co.uk

STUDIO

'Once there was a man who ... pushed a block of ice across a vast city until it melted and disappeared; an artist who sent a peacock to take his place in an important gathering of his peers; a man who persuaded a small army of workers to move an immense sand dune armed only with shovels; a solitary walker who one day emerged from a shop holding a loaded pistol...'

Ruth Hedges talks to artist Jim Lambie in his Glasgow studio. Portrait by Luke Watson

Jim Lambie is back home from New York. Home after a three-year 'affaire' with the Big Apple, he has returned to his Glasgow base, the studio located on Tobermoo Street in the now famous building inhabited by the Modern Institute and many of its artists. The place is ironically 'New York to feel – it affords the escapee, dodging into life shafts. That and an odd Victorian institution.

Maybe it is the latter that is making me feel nervous as I peer along the empty corridors trying to find the right door. A tall, skinny, cool-headed man answers one knock and I apologise to Toby Paterson when ask him off in the right direction.

Jim Lambie's most famous working style – eye-convincing razor-sheened money-theatrical stripes of tape – suggests an obsessive, ordered mind. On quiet, scuffed-up, uneasy man I meet at first doesn't quite tally with this picture. In the big white room that's spattered with green paint from recent work sent to an art fair in Miami we don't know where to sit – a tube is turned on and the roll and we end up building – not a play in cushion, trying to take the edge of the chill. Why did he come back? 'I used to go to NY quite a lot – DJ ma three-and party and it was great,' he says. 'But then when I zoned there, you realise there's a Monday, Tuesday,

Wednesday as well. And then you set in to shred, and it seems to get bigger, to an inner avenue. Lots of people coming and going, usually it's agenda down, there's nobody out there just to be there. So he's happy to be back? Yes, I'm glad to be here in Glasgow and get about some real friends.

At first the penny dropped, ha-lighting illuminates each white wall and floor that start looking and breathing of materials we do not see now. Next to the sofa I'm sitting on, shelves are overflowing with black masking tape. That's still a hangover from his time where I managed to order tea and tape. We calculated a little bit, so there's still a lot hanging around, he says. 'If you ever need masking tape, I'm your man. I got it from a company called Vet Sugar about ten miles from here. They do all the cutting for me, the tape comes in breaks that we I need to get, it comes has its different colours.

Now the ideas stacks of various pile up from a show in Düsseldorf, the ones that didn't make the cut. Runs of chairs line one edge, waiting it feel like a village hall share, dusty towers of card boxes we yet material, red for playing and a glitter ball twinkles in the corner. Over by the shelf of paper, pictures from magazines are stuck on the wall and Elvis leans down in orange glory.

The studio for Lambie is, then, more of a big storage space. Because I make a lot of work on site and so I glib to inject. There's only so much I can prepare here, unless I've got a boss who collects the show, then the shin's going to position itself. As says. But a lot of it is much more term bits by trucking each shape where the chassis, so it's not really the kind of studio based work we where things go place, gallery – it's a site, I would say maybe 30 per cent of the work is made in the studio.

The Modern Institute is one from year and a very large to major international force (director Toby Webster was the only Scottish gallerist to be voted in Art Review's Top 100 most influential people on the art-world), to inherit like, regularly punching up above its weight – from that view as the form of Mohammed Ali. So how did Lambie get involved? 'It was never really anything that was discussed, it was just a case of me re-doing this – do you want to be a part of it?' he says. There's a kind of natural involvement in what's going on. Toby was setting up that space and I was in to helping, it was simple as that. We were just all organising. I didn't really know what he was doing. I knew what he was thinking about but I didn't really know what the potential was or even what he does and sat unison was. If you buy.

I wonder how this relationship works, now that both parties have grown to greater proportions. 'It's not that I feel like some kind of steward of the gallery or anything, it's just handy,' he says. 'It's just there and it is easier actually – questions and calls and if I need to order a material, they can call and sorted for me. Plus it was you their phone space.

And I say you couldn't say that for New York. The top working storage cupboard at number 14 may not be glamorous but it is full of Lambie's stuff. The prodigal son comes back, but Lambie looks set to be back in his odd white room full of artistic leftovers and untidy file cabinets. He's home.

Ruth Hedges is deputy editor of Map.

Luke Watson is an Edinburgh-based photographer. His portraits of prominent figures representing all major paths in Scotland were commissioned and shown at the Scottish National Portrait Gallery, September 2004 – February 2005.

SÃO
PAOLO

W

Dan Flavin
Washington DC

grotesque visions of railway architecture, a mishmash of Otto Wagner urbanity and bizarre Gothick fantasy, complete with verbose quotes from an unknown source. Whether capacious or designed, both this and 'Morris, I got burned', on the opposite wall, are funny in a big fright (but kind of wry a-marriage-of-the-avant-garde and Koch.

At the back of the first room, Piper's *Double Door* divides the usually open-plan (or at least open door) gallery into two separate spaces by means of swinging saloon doors. The centre of the doors is pierced by a cut-out star shape, which serves to frame the fixed, smiling face of the endlessly hula-hooping woman in 'Loop'. Maurice Doherty's double-sided video projection in the room beyond. The doors, unmistakably celluloid-inspired, are such that the temptation to burst, rather than walk through, is hard to resist, and gallery etiquette is put at risk by the potential actions of wannabe cowboys.

This feast of Saturnalia may not be as licentious as its Roman precedent, but it's similarly implicit, peppered with visual raillery and, like W G Sebald's *Glück* which shares its title, the *Rings of Saturn* might well be a meditation on the possibly restorative powers of art.

Susannah Thompson is an art writer and lecturer at Glasgow School of Art

Changing Room Gallery
3 Nov – 12 Dec 2004

Dan Flavin's was once reputed a difficult art: a fact difficult to grasp retrospectively when it can be seen for its sheer beauty. Should we now try to recapture the old sense of obduracy and negation, or rather give ourselves over to the visual fascination exercised by Flavin's bundles of light? Walking through the National Gallery, where Flavin's retrospective premiered before moving on to Fort Worth, then an international tour set to continue through 2007, it's easy to decide on the second course. The installation is ravishing, and the artist's ever-increasing mastery of his chosen medium, whole and coloured fluorescent light in real architectural space, becomes patent as one follows his progress: from the early 'icons' (Johnsian painted monochrome boxes mounted with fluorescent or, more often, incandescent bulbs) through the inaugural pure fluorescent

piece, 'the diagonal of May 25, 1963 (to Constantin Brancusi)' – a eureka point in Flavin's story comparable to, say, 'Onement I' (1948), in Barnett Newman's – marking the moment of greatest conceivable reduction or contraction (the Kabalistic *zimzum* that gave its name to one of Newman's sculptures) in which it momentarily seemed that 'little artistic craft could be possible' but from which all further creation would proceed. And then the polychromatic mixes with which Flavin began experimenting in 1964 but which really took off (richness and complexity around 1970, when Flavin made 'untitled

(to Barnett Newman) to commemorate his simple problem, red, yellow, and blue)'. As shown by this corner construction with its vertical red and blue lights facing away from the open space and back toward the wall, while the horizontal yellow fluorescent tubes face outward, the 'simple' combination of three primary colours as they interfuse in space becomes something almost ungraspable, and indeed escapes language altogether with revealing colour combinations: no longer nameable red, yellow, or blue.

What this indicates is that difficulty remains secreted within the suave beauty of Flavin's 'propositions' – an intellectual rather than an emotional difficulty, at least for the viewer. All the more curious, then, that it should have taken such an irascible character to produce this work. Although Flavin famously wrote of his material as 'common light repeated effulgently across anybody's wall' and of his subject as 'a neutral pleasure of seeing known to everyone', he was in fact notably possessive, one might even say illiberally close-fisted about the notion of his art, compulsively but always eloquently 'deflecting away from the methodological comprehension of his work', as Jack Burnham put it. Whereas most artists seem to believe that their work will unfold itself through time to reveal unforeseeable meaning, Flavin mused of leaving 'a will and testament to declare everything void at my death ... because only I know this work as it ought to be.' All posthumous interpretations are less. 'Robert Morris, of course, had already made "Statement of Aesthetic Withdrawal" (1963) removing 'all esthetic quality and content' from a previous work of his but the result was the addition of a new work, not the subtraction of an existing one from what. Arthur C. Danto was about to dub 'the art world' – meaning, not the social milieu of artists, dealers, collectors, and so on, but the realm of things accepted at a given point in history as belonging to art. No more could Flavin have asserted the ultimate control over the artistic existence of his work by this supreme and sovereign act of disowning it, yet he needed to believe in such controls in order to produce something fine enough to escape it. His art's posthumous existence cannot be switched off like an electric light; despite all the situational uncertainties that surround the effort to represent the effects he sought, the work continues to shine forth, expansively.

Barry Schwabsky is an art critic and author of The Widening Circle: Consequences of Modernism in Contemporary Art (Cambridge University Press) and Opera: Poems 1981–2002 (San Francisco: Meritage Press)

National Gallery of Art Washington DC
3 Oct 2004 – 9 Jan 2005

Left: 'The diagonal of May 25, 1963 (to Constantin Brancusi)'
Dan Flavin, 1963

56

Mat Collishaw
Edinburgh

Mat Collishaw flatters to deceive. His best-known work takes the form of exquisite photographs of flowers whose petals, on closer inspection, have been electronically replaced by close-ups of human skin diseases. Alongside these are his video installations: in one example, a video projection onto an ornate free-standing vanity mirror, depicting a beautiful young girl brushing her long blonde locks, fades into an image of what might well be the same girl 75 years later, still brushing, brushing, brushing her hair. Elsewhere, it's the deceptive power of the medium itself that interests Collishaw: an image of prisoners of the Abu Ghraib prison camp in Iraq is embedded in the form of a room-sized mosaic – in which a highly pixellated internet image provides the pattern for a craft form that originated in Persia, and provided the spoils of war is a different age.

Collishaw's largest solo exhibition to date is located in the beautifully restored Inverleith House, and it comes at an important time for an artist who – amazingly – emerged from the epicentre of Young British Art without having been ripped apart by the media. How could Tracey Emin's (now ex) long-term lover have avoided the same tabloid mauling that was the daily grind for Tracey, Damien, Sarah and Gillian for so much of the past decade? Maybe it is precisely because the work is so hard to pin down. It can be so wilfully artificial that it feels resistant, even at times slippery.

Looking at a projection of blurry photos of victims of Operation Barbarossa lying dead in the frozen Russian winter, you steel yourself for some grim thoughts about the atrocities of the German-Russian war in the early 1940s. But no sooner have you prepared yourself for this emotional onslaught,

than the image literally fizzles and melts away, as if the transparency inside the slide projector has just been destroyed by the heat. Again and again a grimy fuzzy image bubbles into oblivion, just as its content is becoming clear. It is hard to trust your judgement in Collishaw's work, because there's always a sense that, once you succumb to the sheer power or beauty of what you first see, that emotional response will be undermined by the realisation that things are definitely not what they first seemed.

In the end Collishaw's work frustrates because, despite its often very powerful ideas, it doesn't allow the viewer enough room in the work to engage with the artist's vision. Certainly, there's a sense that Collishaw's interests are sharply political. Yet by dickering about with the medium, he undermines the complexity of his message. Again and again he reminds us that what we see may not actually be the whole truth – but in the process each time he gives the impression that, when we get anywhere near his heartfelt convictions, he doesn't in fact hold them at all.

Staring at the Infectious Orchid photographs with their skin-diseased petals, I found myself trying to think of something other than this brisk aphorism, 'beauty is only skin-deep', and wishing I could get to an understanding of his passions that went a little deeper.

Nick Barley is editor of The List

Inverleith House
15 Jan – 13 Mar 2005

Andy Warhol:
Self Portraits
Edinburgh

'He was always such a strong, strong man/ I saw him go to pieces/ I saw him go to pieces'

'Pieces of a Man' – Gil Scott Heron's 1971 hymn to his disenfranchised father could well have been penned after wandering the rooms housing this remarkably complete collection of Warhol's self portraits. Following a trajectory of gauche vulgarity, enthusiasm and playfulness through his portraits move to a final reduction of form that, like the man himself in his later years, is almost translucent. At his best and worst Warhol was gifted and truly godless in his experimentation and this superb exhibition runs the gamut of the pope of pop art's (self) reflections and creativity.

Opening with Warhol's early childish but oddly effective graphite on paper sketches, his influence on future artists, even as a boy, can be identified in a drawing of Clint Hamilton, Nathan Gluck and himself (nicely stained with what looks like coffee). This graphite and coloured pencil sketch on Strathmore paper can now be seen as the reference point for a composition to which fellow artists; David Hockney and Dennis Hopper (as photographers) frequently returned.

What follows next serves to illustrate what a funny, silly and joyful artist Warhol could be. His youthful visage bursts out of blue, pink and yellow acrylic screen prints; in some he looks like the Jackal, in others like blonde

Above left: 'Burning Flower'
Mat Collishaw, 2004
Left: Early Self-Portrait
Andy Warhol, 1986

57

Issue 1/Spring 2005/**MAP**

Certain of

NOTHING:

150_151

ZERO
Dunraven Student Magazine

ARE SCHOOL DINNERS GETTING BETTER?

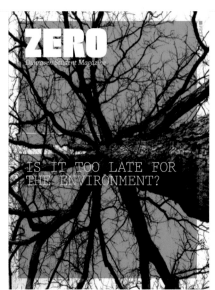

ZERO
Dunraven Student Magazine

IS IT TOO LATE FOR THE ENVIRONMENT?

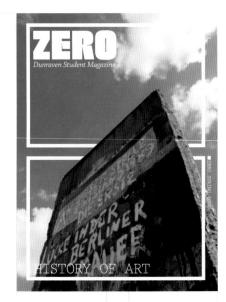

ZERO
Dunraven Student Magazine

HISTORY OF ART

Welcome to Zero, issue one of our new magazine. Within these pages are the opinions, ideas and interests of the students of this fine institution. We hope you will also be contributing, at: **zeromagazine@duravenschool.org.uk**

The project itself is the brainchild of previous students of the school and was conceived almost three years ago as part of the joinedupdesignforschools programme, a national project. In late 2006 the editorial and design teams that have worked so hard to bring this magazine to you were formed.

Studio8 Design worked with the student design team and have come up with an original and professional concept which gave us the name "Zero". As you can see the page numbers form the layout of the page and the front cover was page "Zero".

This issue of the magazine feature articles on Chinese New Year, a feature on size zero models and the obscure, intense, Afgan sport of Buzkashi.

Truman Wright, Yr 10

AROUND TOWN
Places to go on your days off

Friday 30th March 2007
Gilbert & George exhibition at Tate modern

Monday 16th April 2007
Fortnum & Masons Tea

Monday 7th May 2007
Bloomsbury Bowling Alley

30th March 2007
Gilbert & George bring their large scale controversial work to the Tate Modern. Don't be put however, by the bad press: even if you think its s**t the work is worth seeing for the sheer power of the images. www.tate.org.uk/modern

Monday 16th April
Well, how about a spot of tea at Fortnum & Mason? Fortnum & Mason you say? But that's for archdukes and wealthy Cypriots or those who get fifty million pound Christmas bonuses. Correct if one is wishing to purchase a three course meal with Beluga Caviar and a one hundred and ten pound bottle of 1977 Tailor Vintage Port, but, if you only want an ice cream sundae it will not dent your pocket by more than about 23 pounds. www.fortnumandmason.com

Monday 7th May 2007
Situated in the classy center of London, the Bloomsbury Bowling Alley provides an experience well above the of the grotty Megabowl. With authentic imported American furnishings, a vintage cinema and shoes worthy of any 50s sitcom, a great atmosphere fill the place. It's cheap to (on Mondays) and the food is deliciously authentic. www.bloomsburybowling.com

And Weekends
Don't be alarmed, there are more than three days off for the entirity of next year, so we have come up with a list of other choses faire. Here they are: Brick Lane for bric-a-brac, records and the heigth of fashion. Go to the countryside, a coach trip to Oxford can cost as little as £1 and as a large number of people in the school have never experienced the joys of out-of-city life it is a fantastic thing to do. Brighton by train, includes shops, markets and fish and chips.
www.visitbricklane.com; www.eastlondonmarkets.com www.oxfordcity.co.uk; www.nationalexpress.com www.brighton.co.uk

Oscar Taylor & William Elliott, Yr 10

Above: Brighton's attractions exert their pull

Below: Gilbert and George, a menacing epic

Welcome to Zero, issue one of our new magazine. Within these pages are the opinions, ideas and interests of the students of this fine institution. We hope you will also be contributing, at: **zeromagazine@duravenschool.org.uk**

The project itself is the brainchild of previous students of the school and was conceived almost three years ago as part of the joinedupdesignforschools programme, a national project. In late 2006 the editorial and design teams that have worked so hard to bring this magazine to you were formed.

Studio8 Design worked with the student design team and have come up with an original and professional concept which gave us the name "Zero". As you can see the page numbers form the layout of the page and the front cover was page "Zero".

This issue of the magazine feature articles on Chinese New Year, a feature on size zero models and the obscure, intense, Afgan sport of Buzkashi.

Truman Wright, Yr 10

ZERO. SUMMER. 2007

AROUND TOWN
Places to go on your days off

EVENTS

Friday 30th March 2007
Gilbert & George exhibition at Tate modern

Monday 16th April 2007
Fortnum & Masons Tea

Monday 7th May 2007
Bloomsbury Bowling Alley

30th March 2007
Gilbert and George bring their large scale controversial work to the Tate Modern. Don't be put however, by the bad press even if you think it's s**t the work is worth seeing for the sheer power of the images. www.tate.org.uk/modern

Monday 16th April
Well, how about a spot of tea at Fortnum & Mason? Fortnum & Mason you say? But that's for archdukes and wealthy Cypriots or those who get fifty million pound Christmas bonuses. Correct if one is wishing to purchase a three course meal with Beluga Caviar and a one hundred and ten pound bottle of 1977 Tailor Vintage Port, but, if you only want an ice cream sundae it will not dent your pocket by more than about 23 pounds. www.fortnumandmason.com

Monday 7th May 2007
Situated in the classy center of London, the Bloomsbury Bowling Alley provides an experience well above the rise of the grotty Megabowl. With authentic imported American furnishings, a vintage cinema and shoes worthy of any 50s sitcom, a great atmosphere fills the place. It's cheap to (on Mondays) and the food is fabulously authentic. www.bloomsburybowling.com

And Weekends
Don't be alarmed, there are more than three days off for the entirety of next year, so we have come up with a set of other cheese finds. Here they are: Brick Lane for bric-a-brac, records and the length of fashion. Go to the countryside, a coach trip to Oxford can cost as little as £1 and as a large number of people in the school have never experienced the joys of out-of-city life it is a fantastic thing to do. Brighton by train, includes shops, markets and fish and chips.
www.visitbricklane.com www.eastlondonmarkets.com
www.oxfordcity.co.uk www.nationalexpress.com
www.brighton.co.uk

Oscar Taylor & William Elliot, Yr 10

Below: Gilbert and George, a menacing epic

Above: Brighton's attractions exert their pull

ZERO. SUMMER. 2007

GRID SPECIFICATIONS

Page size (trimmed)	205 x 275mm
Top margin	17mm
Bottom margin	18.06mm
Outside margin	20.492mm
Inside margin	17mm
Number of columns	4
Gutter width	10.5mm
Extras	Baseline grid, 10pt

ZERO: DUNRAVEN STUDENT MAGAZINE
Design: Matt Willey and Zoë Bather at Studio8 Design

Zero is the Dunraven Secondary School termly magazine. It was commissioned by the Sorrell Foundation, which links designers and students in collaborative projects to improve the quality of life in schools. Designers Matt Willey and Zoë Bather worked closely with the pupils, to create a template that would be easy for them to use as editorial content was developed. The system is based around large folio numbers which fill each page. These count up from zero on the front cover, and create a set of different-shaped spaces into which the students drop the content. This rigid and explicit grid ensures that the students' layouts are consistent and professional, and gives a strong identity to the magazine.

CONTEMPORARY KALEIDOSCOPE

Kathy Battista surveys autumn highlights from the energetic British contemporary art scene

WILDER WEST

Rumours of the demise of the West End, long a bastion of the art trade, have been exaggerated. Recently, something of a renaissance has been taking place, with galleries such as Spruth Magers Lee, Riflemaker, Blow de la Barra, Waddington Galleries and Annely Juda fighting back with an impressive array of exhibitions this autumn. Catch painters Richard Patterson at Timothy Taylor Gallery, and Federico Herrero at Blow de la Barra, and installation artist Jason Rhoades at Hauser & Wirth.

Not to be missed is Haunch of Venison's show of the late American artist Edward Kienholz and his wife Nancy Reddin Kienholz (7 Oct–9 Nov), known for their disturbing sculptural installations (below). The show features pieces from their recent joint retrospective at Baltic, including anti-war works, and new work previously unseen in the UK.

FRANCIS ALŸS

This enigmatic artist Francis Alÿs turned walking into an art form. Born in Antwerp, and now working in Mexico City, Alÿs sees the city as a huge open-air studio and makes work, such as animations, poetic films and paintings, that map cities in elusive ways. Over the past five years, he has walked the streets of London to create a new project for Artangel, called 'Seven Walks' (28 Sep–20 Nov), which explores the everyday rituals of the metropolis – from Coldstream Guards (below) to London's commuters. The show also provides a rare glimpse of one of London's most stunning buildings: Robert Adam's eighteenth-century townhouse in Portman Square, now a private club.

BRITISH ART SHOW 6

The British Art Show, which takes place every five years, provides an important opportunity to take the pulse of contemporary art in the UK. Each show selects a group of artists to represent the diversity and range of British art. This year, the show starts at Baltic (24 Sep–8 Jan 2006), the revamped flourmill in Gateshead that has changed the face of the contemporary art scene in the North. Organised by London's Hayward Gallery and selected by independent curators Andrea Schlieker and Alex Farquharson, the exhibition features 49 of the most important emerging artists now working in Britain. Look out for Haluk Akakçe (below) and Saskia Olde Wolbers, both masters of digital and video installation. Other highlights include Juneau/Projects, an artists collective who examine technology's role in consumer culture, and French-born Zineb Sedira, an artist with Algerian roots, who explores cultural identity. If you miss the Baltic show, there is still a chance to see it as it tours to Manchester, Nottingham and Bristol.

This page, clockwise from left: 'The Bronze Pinball Machine with Woman Affixed Also', 1980, by Ed & Nancy Kienholz; 'Seven Walks', 2005, by Francis Alÿs; 'The Birth of Art', 2003, by Haluk Akakçe and 'It was hard to believe that at 24 he was sitting at my desk wrestling with the next round of deadlines', 2004, by Matthew Houlding (both in British Art Show 6).

WAY OUT EAST

London's East End has become an established hub of contemporary art. With a combination of existing venues such as White Cube – showing the Chapman brothers' new work this autumn (19 Oct–3 Dec) – and newcomers such as Herald Street and David Risley, East London offers endless opportunities for seeing new art. Highlights this autumn include paintings by the duo Muntean/Rosenblum at Maureen Paley's Interim Art, and Susanne Kühn at a new space called Fred. At Paul Stolper's gallery (13 Oct–19 Nov), Damien Hirst creates a chapel-like installation where religion meets pharmaceuticals, with an altar, a cedar cross and 40 newly commissioned silkscreen prints.

A particular highlight this autumn is a show of Isaac Julien's films at Victoria Miro Gallery (14 Oct–12 Nov). Julien is a master of creating impeccably crafted, lush film installations that focus on the impact of location – both cultural and physical. Victoria Miro Gallery will also host the UK premiere of two new films: *True North* (below), about Matthew Henson, the first African-American to reach the North Pole; and *Fantôme Afrique*, shot in the arid spaces of rural Burkina Faso, and features rich imagery of urban Ouagadougou, the centre for cinema in Africa.

Opposite, clockwise from left: 'True North Series', 2004, by Isaac Julien; 'Whiteout, implant, scale', 2004, by Anish Kapoor; RA: 'Untitled', 2004, by Cindy Sherman; 'Roundup – An Entomological Endeavour for the Smart Museum of Art', 2000, by Mark Dion; 'Work No. 329 – Half the Air in a Given Space', 2004, by Martin Creed.

FRIEZE (AND OTHER) ART FAIRS

The Frieze Art Fair (20–24 Oct), established two years ago, has become one of the most important events in London's contemporary art calendar. It hosts 150 galleries (selected from a field of over 450) from around the world in an elaborate tent in Regent's Park, designed by the young British architect David Adjaye. In addition to providing the opportunity to see and buy cutting-edge art, Frieze also hosts events, including talks, a music programme and high-profile public arts commissions. Peckish art-lovers are also well-catered for – the café menu has been created by Mark Hix, of The Ivy and Le Caprice.

Last year saw the birth of two satellite events around Frieze – Zoo Art Fair, located in Regent's Park Zoo, and Scope London in the Meliá White House hotel just outside the park. Limited to UK-based galleries less than three years old, Zoo presents more experimental work than the grown-up fair and is an opportunity to see up-and-coming talent. Look out for RA graduate Francesca Lowe's exquisite and delicate paintings at Riflemaker's stand.

Meanwhile, Scope London, a fair that also takes place in Miami, New York and L.A. has had the bright idea of asking galleries to set up shop in their hotel rooms. By combining the costs of travel and exhibiting, international galleries can take the work of relatively young and affordable, emerging artists on the road.

NORTH/SOUTH

This autumn, art lovers need to go off the Thames for two shows that are not to be missed. The South London Gallery presents Microcosmographia by American artist Mark Dion (until 30 Oct), a fantastic nature-inspired sculptural world inhabited by gigantic creatures, including a life-size replica of an Ichthyosaur, a prehistoric aquatic animal, considered to be the Tyrannosaurus rex of the sea.

In North London, Camden Arts Centre presents Runa Islam and Roderick Buchanan (23 Sep–13 Nov). The show includes Islam's *First Day of Spring*, a film featuring rickshaw drivers in Dhaka, and Buchanan's *History Painting*, which looks at soldiers in North Yorkshire and Madras. Elsewhere in North London, dealer Simon Gillespie has turned his Georgian townhouse in Islington into a contemporary art gallery, Rollo. This autumn he shows the atmospheric landscape work of Korean photographer Bae Bien-U (29 Sep–3 Nov).

China

CHINESE WHISPERS

Edvard Munch

BENEATH THE SKIN

Grids: Creative Solutions for Graphic Designers

GRID SPECIFICATIONS

Page size (trimmed)	230 x 300mm
Top margin	20mm
Bottom margin	16mm
Outside margin	10mm
Inside margin	18mm
Number of columns	12
Gutter width	4mm
Extras	Baseline grid, 11pt

RA MAGAZINE

Design: Matt Willey and Zoë Bather at Studio8 Design

The redesign of the *RA Magazine* was a particularly challenging job. It was established 25 years ago, has the largest circulation of any art magazine in Europe, and represents a major institution. The readership of the magazine demands clear navigation with clean, elegant design, but designer Matt Willey also wanted "to put time and craft into making pages that were dynamic and expressive." Willey believes that grids can be restrictive and, especially within editorial design, can prevent pages from looking interesting if followed too religiously. In this design he employs a flexible multi-column structure so that his designs are respectful of content, yet a little playful as well.

ENTER THE DRAGON

A NATURAL PHENOMENON

WE'LL ALWAYS HAVE
PARIS

MAN OF MYSTERY

Painter Humphrey Ocean RA is a rather elusive character. As he treats *Sarah Greenberg* to tales of his rock and roll past and love of Raymond Chandler, he reveals clues to his art and life. Photograph by *Julian Anderson*

TO BE PERFECTLY FRANK

Newly elected Academician Frank Bowling picks up his brushes and paints as he talks to *James Cahill* in his new, much loftier studio. Photograph by *Eamonn McCabe*

NAKED AMBITION

Amedeo Modigliani's sensuous nudes and portraits are as captivating as the artist's legendary life story, argues *Kenneth Wayne*

Grids: Creative Solutions for Graphic Designers

THE CLASS OF 06

In a class of their own The RA Schools final-year students showcase their art this summer. On the following pages, photographer *Nick Cunard* visits their studios to capture the spirit of the young artists at work. Here *Maurice Cockrill RA*, Keeper of the RA Schools, explains what makes the place so special and praises the outgoing graduates

HOWARD'S WAY

TREASURES

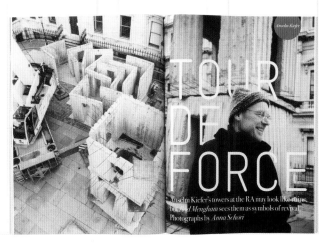

TOUR DE FORCE

Anselm Kiefer's towers at the RA may look like ruins, but *Rod Mengham* sees them as symbols of revival
Photographs by *Anna Schori*

1921
PREMIUM DENIM

86 years is a long time to perfect the art of jean craftsmanship. Fortunately 1921 Premium Denim have mastered it and are now bringing their cult LA jeans to London. Denim brand fads are often more fleeting than runway trends themselves, but as one of the oldest family-owned denim manufacturers in the world, heritage and endurance is something they clearly understand. Using Italian or Japanese denim, each piece is handcrafted, treated, washed and then finished with a special abrasion technique ensuring every pair is unique, and characterised by a vintage style finish. Not just lovingly crafted, but with a conscience too: all denim is spun from ecologically sound cotton. ●

If the metal leggings are just a little too 7km for you, one can still indulge in Nicholas Ghesquiere's feminine and mid-futurism, with Balenciaga's first ever eyewear range. Echoing the space cadet look for his spring/summer '07 ready-to-wear collection, the eyewear line is a first for Ghesquiere at the Parisian house.

Large transparent framed wrap arounds, house grey or yellow reflective lenses with giant chrome studs on the arms. Cyber-goggles they're not, just being bug-eyed has never been so chic.

Influenced heavily by sci-fi, this was Ghesquiere's first turkoir flirtation with the future – spurning plundering the archives of Cristobal like he's done in previous seasons. Decidedly creating his own legacy at Balenciaga, rather than just seizing the Spanish designers' radically formed silhouettes.

Think today, tomorrow, and what may be. Are the days of designers pilfering the past for inspiration gone? The future is now. ●

BALENCIAGA

SANDRA BACKLUND

Swedish knitwear genius Sandra Backlund incorporated human hair into her first collection of architectural, madcap knits. That phase has passed and she is now using only the richest red wools instead. A knitwear couturier, Backlund plays with structure, creating outlandish tulip skirts, massive shoulders and kooky headgear. Not a Purl knit in sight, thank God, just futuristic sculptures that manage to retain romance and femininity in their shapes. Her inventiveness has earnt her a place in knitting's renaissance. ●

TOM FORD

The tanned Texan responsible for putting the sex back into Gucci is launching his first solo store in New York. 845 Madison Avenue, Manhattan is to be the home of the new TOM FORD signature menswear collection, which will include, RTW, footwear and eyewear. "My aim is to address an extremely discerning luxury customer who demands the highest quality product and service," claims Ford.

Fortunately for disciples of his suave and polished chic, he's plans to spread his wings over the next few years – opening stores in Milan, London, LA and Tokyo. ●

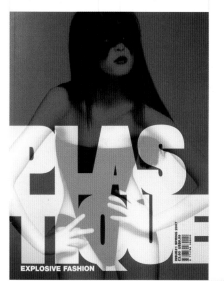

PLAS TIQUE
EXPLOSIVE FASHION

ISSUE 4 SPRING 2007
£3.40 US$6.99

WHEN JODIE MET AMANDA

A CONVERSATION WITH AMANDA LEPORE

"I've known Amanda for a few years now. Before I met her for the first time, I expected a terrifying diva, perhaps reminiscent of Pete Burns. In the flesh, away from the camp, exaggerated images of her, in LaChapelle, she is stunning. The moment I first met her, on an interview assignment for a magazine, my expectations were pleasantly shattered. When she answered the door to her hotel room in the East Village, NYC (the same room she'd lived in for a decade) with a big smile on her face and a kiss on the cheek, we bonded immediately over lipsticks and hairpieces.

What Amanda has done to her body and what I do to mine are two contrasting things. My body work is clubs and gay and I look glamorous for the cameras but I'm happy being a boy who dresses up for a living, and for fun not for sexual reasons. Amanda, who has an often publicly flaunted vagina, was born Armand. She has used her looks, gender re-assignment surgery, cosmetic surgery, silicone injections, make-up and fashion to fabulantly turned into the 'Number One Transsexual in the World' ®, and deserves ultimate respect for it. There is quite possibly no-one else who has worked so much on their physical appearance and boy-does-this-woman-work-it.

Photograph **Ben Charles Edwards**
Words **Jodie Harsh**

Grids: Creative Solutions for Graphic Designers

GRID SPECIFICATIONS

Page size (trimmed)	220 x 285mm
Top margin	15mm
Bottom margin	15mm
Outside margin	10mm
Inside margin	20mm
Number of columns	12
Gutter width	4mm
Extras	Baseline grid, 11pt

PLASTIQUE

Design: Matt Willey and Matt Curtis at Studio8 Design

Plastique is a quarterly women's fashion magazine. The basic elements of its design are very simple. There are two headline fonts; one text font, also used for the captions; and a 12-column grid that is frequently ignored! Designers Matt Willey and Matt Curtis wanted to work with as few rules as possible so that pages are designed as much through instinct as preconceived logic. The largely monochromatic color scheme was chosen to suit the ballsy and unapologetic nature of the magazine. As Willey says, "we didn't want anything too clinical, too fluffy, too saccharine, too girly."

Grids: Creative Solutions for Graphic Designers

B1

GREAT
EASTERN
STREET
PHOTOGRAPHY
DAVID DUNAN

EDITORS ADDRESS

THIS IS IT.
CREATIVITY.
BRAVERY.
FEARLESSNESS.
LIFE IS A JOURNEY.
SO IS PLASTIQUE.
THINK
FOR
YOURSELF.

BRYLIE QUINN FOWLER

ZERO DEGREES

PHOTOGRAPHY JEFFREY GRATTON

KILLAH KOLOR

PHOTOGRAPHY
JOHN LINDQUIST

AGGRESSORIES

URBAN ARMOUR –
FASHIONISTAS ARM THEMSELVES FOR
EVERYDAY BATTLE

DAY 2

DAY 3

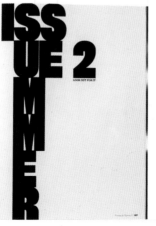

ISSUE 2

LOOK OUT FOR IT

SUBSCRIBE NOW!

RECEIVE FOUR ISSUES A YEAR AND AS EXCLUSIVE (AS M.B
LEATHER FOLDER, HAND EMBOSSED WITH THE PLASTIQUE LOGO

GO TO WWW.PLASTIQUEMAGAZINE.COM

CANADIAN EXPORT

DRAGONETTE BRINGS PLASTIQUE
INTO THEIR WORLD OF ELECTRO-
POP ORGIES

13.10.05
RIBA STIRLING
PRIZE

AJ

THE ARCHITECTS' JOURNAL WWW.AJPLUS.CO.UK

£3.25

ISSN 0003-8466

9 770003 846103

THE FASCINATION WITH
SURFACE GIVES THIS MOST
BASIC OF BUILDING TYPES
AN INTELLIGENCE AND
ENQUIRY THAT IS PALPABLE

CONTENTS

SUBSCRIBE

CONTENTS

P. 14
ZAHA HADID

P. 25
TRANSPORT INTERCHANGE

P. 46
JAN KAPLICKY

P. 12
SAATCHI GALLERY

P. 16
MAKE

P. 58
TONY FRETTON

GRID SPECIFICATIONS

Page size (trimmed)	210 x 265mm
Top margin	12mm
Bottom margin	12mm
Outside margin	12mm
Inside margin	12mm
Number of columns	4
Gutter width	4mm
Extras	Baseline grid, 3.883mm

AJ: THE ARCHITECTS' JOURNAL

Design: APFEL (A Practice for Everyday Life) with Sarah Douglas

APFEL redesigned *The Architects' Journal* in collaboration with Sarah Douglas. Together they developed a clean and simple design so that architectural process and progress are foregrounded. The grid is a simple four-column structure, and is used discreetly. Spreads look considered without being precious so that layouts can happily accommodate ephemeral content and at the same time showcase finished work. Images can be full bleed or squared up, and at times overlap or appear to hang from a top rule as though pinned on a wall. Folios, running feet, and rules at the top and bottom of each page quietly establish the overall page architecture.

Redefining Green-ness

Green-ness is the obscure object of desire that has been driving the development of suburbia since its beginnings. People fled to suburbia to get away from the congested city and its dense housing blocks, polluted air and car-dominated public space. The endless plains of fields and woods became a utopian image countering the urban dystopia of continuously built fabric. But as city dwellers started to migrate into suburbia, they brought with them their civilised baggage from the city and inevitably dumped it wherever they chose to settle anew. Hence the longing image of green landscape that was the reason for most suburbanites to come here in the first place was replaced over time, the difference being that people now had no other place left to go in order to find what they were looking for.

It is this paradox that the projects assembled here attempt to tackle. Common to all is the thesis that the degradation of landscape in suburbia is caused by a constant misunderstanding, and misuse, of green space. In today's suburbia, green space is, in fact, only very rarely staged to complement the built fabric with landscape. In most cases it serves a completely different objective, namely the provision of privacy. Hence the insurpassable importance of the front garden, which is basically a set-back space texture-mapped with green lawn.

To satisfy both desires, the schemes presented here propose to deal with them separately. Privacy, on the one hand, is achieved by raising the house in the air (Greenurbia) or sinking it in the ground (Sub-'burb), which in return frees up ground space for other uses, for instance public programmes. On the other hand, landscape is maintained by programming parts of the site with non-building programmes such as parks, gardens or agricultural uses (Fischbek-Mississippi) or by introducing a strong topographical definition (Sonic Polder).

46

47

DEEP PLANNING
West Side, New York

Ben Van Berkel and Caroline Bos have devised an urban strategy of 'deep planning', which responds to New York's needs as an unstable and mutating global city. This competition was sponsored by the arcx and included planning the West Side from 34th Street to 23rd Street. The metropolis is treated as a topology of fluctuating networks rather than distinct organisational units. Using combinations of temporal digital techniques, the project integrates infrastructures, urbanism and various programmes by looking for correspondences and overlaps between the locations and functions involved. This site is thus cast as a lobby for Manhattan, the aim being to respond to, rather than to dictate, patterns of use and function.

Due to their relatively short history there is less pressure on new interventions to comply with the piled-up fabric of the past

Redefining Green-ness

Green-ness is the obscure object of desire that has been driving the development of suburbia since its beginnings. People fled to suburbia to get away from the congested city and its dense housing blocks, polluted air and car-dominated public space. The endless plains of fields and woods became a utopian image countering the urban dystopia of continuously built fabric. But as city dwellers started to migrate into suburbia, they brought with them their civilised baggage from the city and inevitably dumped it wherever they chose to settle anew. Hence the longing image of green landscape that was the reason for most suburbanites to come here in the first place was replaced over time, the difference being that people now had no other place left to go in order to find what they were looking for.
It is this paradox that the projects assembled here attempt to tackle. Common to all is the thesis that the degradation of landscape in suburbia is caused by a constant misunderstanding, and misuse, of green space. In today's suburbia, green space is, in fact, only very rarely staged to complement the built fabric with landscape. In most cases it serves a completely different objective, namely the provision of privacy. Hence the insurpassable importance of the front garden, which is basically a set-back space texture-mapped with green lawn.
To satisfy both desires, the schemes presented here propose to deal with them separately. Privacy, on the one hand, is achieved by raising the house in the air (Greenurbia) or sinking it in the ground (Sub- burb), which in return frees up ground space for other uses, for instance public programmes. On the other hand, landscape is maintained by programming parts of the site with non-building programmes such as parks, gardens or agricultural uses (Fischbek-Mississippi) or by introducing a strong topographical definition (Sonic Polder).

46

47

GRID SPECIFICATIONS

Page size (trimmed)	290 x 220mm
Top margin	25mm
Bottom margin	22mm
Outside margin	15mm
Inside margin	18mm
Number of columns	1, 2, or 4
Gutter width	4mm
Baseline grid	N/A

AD (ARCHITECTURAL DESIGN)

Design: Christian Küsters at CHK Design

Inspired by the Bauhaus, Christian Küsters took the "pure" forms of the square, the circle, and the triangle as his starting point in designing the AD logo. The redesign of the magazine grew out of this approach. The font usage and grid are part of a flexible template developed by Küsters to maximize variety in the content and reflect the different themes of each issue.

ART AND POLITICS

ROGER COOK

THE LOVE THAT DARES TO SPEAK ITS NAME

Clive Sartelle

THE PRINCE

CHAPTER VI

The right-hand column text of The Prince is too small to read reliably.

THE PRINCE
CHAPTER VI

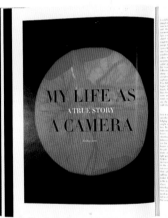

MY LIFE AS
A TRUE STORY
A CAMERA

MERLIN JAMES

FICTIONS OF REPRESENTATION

The work of Merlin James (along with that of some of his near contemporaries) offers an opportunity to examine some pressing issues within representational painting as perceived in the current climate of contemporary art. James's paintings are interesting because they appeal to some generality of perception of what a painting practice should be and while acknowledging a developmental modernist lineage, refuse to sit comfortably within this.

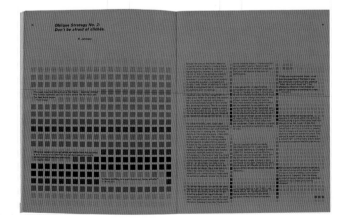

Oblique Strategy No. 2:
Don't be afraid of clichés.
R. Johnson

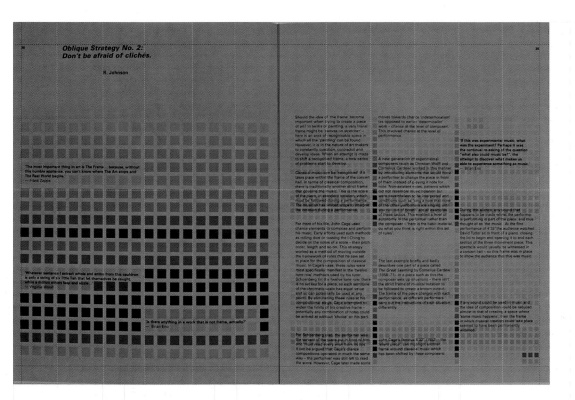

GRID SPECIFICATIONS

Page size (trimmed)	210 x 265mm
Top margin	18.8mm
Bottom margin	18.8mm
Outside margin	7.8mm
Inside margin	5.6mm
Number of columns	6
Gutter width	N/A
Extras	N/A

MISER & NOW

Design: Hannah Dumphy at CHK Design

Miser & Now (an anagram of the publishers' first names—Simon and Andrew) is an occasional visual arts magazine published by the Keith Talent Gallery. Art director Christian Küsters took banknote design as a starting point—a subliminal reminder of the relationship between the finance and fine art markets. Küsters and designer Hannah Dumphy respond to the editorial content of each issue and design accordingly—sometimes there isn't a conventional grid, sometimes each article is designed to fit its page using a flexible grid system, and sometimes opening pages are designed to read more like a poster.

Packaging

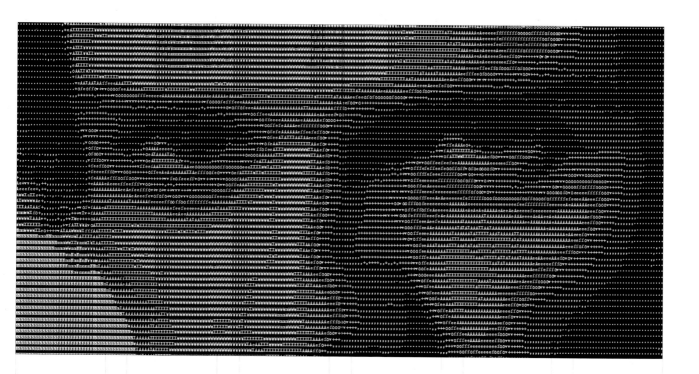

GRID SPECIFICATIONS

Page size (trimmed)	CD inlay: 150 x 117.5mm
	Booklet: 120.65 x 119.89mm
Top margin	N/A
Bottom margin	N/A
Outside margin	N/A
Inside margin	N/A
Number of columns	1
Gutter width	N/A
Extras	Baseline grid, as set by typewriter;
	56 horizontal rows

FREDDIE STEVENSON: A BODY ON THE LINE

Design: Rian Hughes at Device

Although the artwork was, in fact, put together on a Mac, with images created using an ASCII-art program, the overall impression of Rian Hughes' design for this CD packaging is that it is mechanically produced and generally low-tech. Hughes' intention was to echo Stevenson's music visually. Stevenson's music is made with little modern studio equipment, and without the aid of computer trickery. While there is no column grid employed, the type and images utilize a tightly packed series of horizontal lines that give a repetitive structure to the overall design, and increase its mechanical feel.

Adobe Systems Incorporated 2003 Annual Report

Adobe

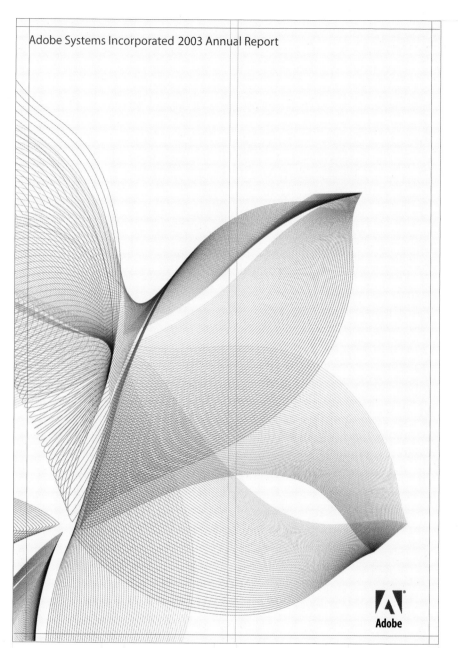

Adobe Systems Incorporated 2003 Annual Report

GRID SPECIFICATIONS

Page size (trimmed)	256.1 x 359.8mm
Top margin	4.939mm
Bottom margin	4.233mm
Outside margin	4.939mm
Inside margin	12.7mm
Number of columns	2
Gutter width	4.233mm
Extras	N/A

ADOBE SYSTEMS INCORPORATED
2003 ANNUAL REPORT
*Design: Julian Bittiner and Brett Wickens
at MetaDesign San Francisco*

The brief for Adobe's 2003 Annual Report
was to highlight the company's heritage
and vision. With this in mind MetaDesign
created a brand framework around three
distinct themes: communicating ideas,
exchanging information, and sharing
memories. Once identified, these themes
determined the design, and MetaDesign
developed a simple, clear typographic and
photographic approach using a traditional
grid structure to underpin its modern-
looking designs.

Adobe Systems Incorporated Corporate overview

Adobe

Adobe Systems Incorporated Corporate overview

Adobe

GRID SPECIFICATIONS

Page size (trimmed)	260.35 x 378.9mm
Top margin	14.817mm
Bottom margin	21.167mm
Outside margin	14mm
Inside margin	14mm
Number of columns	3
Gutter width	4.233mm
Extras	N/A

ADOBE SYSTEMS INCORPORATED
CORPORATE OVERVIEW

Design: Julian Bittiner at MetaDesign
San Francisco

In this brochure, MetaDesign expanded
upon the themes of the Adobe Systems
2003 Annual Report (see pages 176_177).
The overall structure was similar, but
MetaDesign introduced bolder colors;
demonstrative photography, showing
how the applications are used; and large
typographic statements all designed to
convey the dynamism of the company and
reflect its leading brand position.

GRID SPECIFICATIONS

Page size (trimmed)	241 x 233mm
Top margin	8.46mm
Bottom margin	9.87mm
Outside margin	9mm
Inside margin	45mm
Number of columns	5
Gutter width	N/A
Extras	N/A

ADOBE ILLUSTRATOR CS2 PACKAGING

Design: Hui-Ling Chen and Brett Wickens at MetaDesign San Francisco

In 2003, Adobe introduced the Creative Suite and commissioned MetaDesign to help it "emotionally reconnect" with its graphically sophisticated audience by redesigning the packaging and related materials. Artist Nick Veasey, who works in a studio specially equipped for radiography, captured the X-rays used in the packaging and icon system. These images reveal the mathematical formulas that define many forms found in nature—and are often used by designers in developing geometric grid structures. However, although the growth pattern of a shell or the shape of a leaf is determined by a fixed formula, no two shells or leaves are exactly the same—MetaDesign used this as a metaphor to illustrate the variety of results possible when using computer software.

Abbeydale Grange
Specialist Media Arts School
Hastings Road
Sheffield S7 2GU
T 0114 255 7301
F 0114 250 8540
www.abbeydalegrange.co.uk
www.agsmedia.co.uk

GRID SPECIFICATIONS

Page size (trimmed)	1,763 x 160mm
Top margin	20mm
Bottom margin	20mm
Outside margin	20mm
Inside margin	20mm
Number of columns	140
Gutter width	3.131mm
Extras	10 horizontal fields

ABBEYDALE GRANGE IDENTITY

Design: Zoë Bather at Studio8 Design

Abbeydale is one of a number of schools that are involved in the Joinedupdesignforschools initiative run by the Sorrell Foundation. This initiative links designers with schools where the pupils are the commissioning clients. Working closely with the students, Studio8 developed a new visual identity for the school, creating a logo, stationery, signage, posters, brochures, and design guidelines to guarantee effective implementation of the identity. To ensure flexibility and consistency, designer Zoë Bather employed a multi-column structure, further divided into a series of small fields, across the various items. The school's vibrant multiculturalism—over 50 different languages are spoken there—is celebrated in the bright, multicolored graphics.

RAZ OHARA
HYMN MIXES

A1/JAHCOOZI REMIX//A2/RICHARD DAVIS REMIX // B1/RICHARD DAVIS ACID REPRISE//B2/LITWINENKO REMIX//33RPM

ALL TRACKS WRITTEN AND COMPOSED BY PATRICK RASMUSSEN//A1 REMIXED BY ROBOT KOCH/MIXED DOWN BY SREN GERLITZ AT JAHCOOZI STUDIO //A2 AND B1 REMIXES AND ADDITIONAL PRODUCTION BY RICHARD DAVIS//B2 REMIX AND ADDITIONAL PRODUCTION BY LITWINENKO//ALL TRACKS PUBLISHED BY EDITION BIATKLON/BUDDE MUSIKVERLAG//MASTERED BY HELMUT ERLER AT DUBPLATES AND MASTERING/DESIGN BY ALORENZ BERLIN//MANUFACTURED BY HANDLE WITH CARE//WWW.HANDLEWITHCARE.BE/ MADE IN GERMANY/GEMA / LC 02816 // P AND C 2005 KITTY-YO//WWW.KITTY-YO.COM // WORLDWIDE DISTRIBUTION BY INTERGROOVE/FAX 49(0)69-94547555/ORDER NO. CUTS-003-6/THIS IS SIDE B

CHIKINKI
ETHER RADIO REMIXES

A1/ETHER RADIO JAN DRIVER & SIR IUSMO – BOLT REMIX // A2/ASSASSINATOR 13 ED LALIQ'S ALBION CALL REMIX//B1/ETHER RADIO SERGE SANTIAGO VOCAL   45RPM

ALL TRACKS WRITTEN BY CHIKINKI/COPYRIGHT CONTROL//A1 REMIX AND ADDITIONAL PRODUCTION BY JAN DRIVER AND SIRIUSMO/RECORDED AT THE SUPER-SOUND-SUITE BERLIN/JAN DRIVER APPEARS COURTESY OF GRAND PETROL RECORDINGS GERMANY/WWW.GRANDPETROL.INFO//A2 REMIX AND ADDITIONAL PRODUCTION BY E.GURDIS AND M.LANCASTER//B1 REMIX AND ADDITIONAL PRODUCTION BY SERGE SANTIAGO/MASTERED BY LUPO AT DUBPLATES AND MASTERING/DESIGN BY ALORENZ BERLIN//MANUFACTURED BY HANDLE WITH CARE/MADE IN GERMANY/GEMA / LC 02816//A1 AND A2 P AND C 2005 KITTY-YO/WWW.KITTY-YO.COM//B1 P AND C 2004 AND 2005 UNIVERSAL ISLAND RECORDS LTD. UNDER EXCLUSIVE LICENSE TO KITTY-YO / WORLDWIDE DISTRIBUTION BY INTERGROOVE/FAX 49(0)69-94547555/ORDER NO. CUTS-001-6/THIS IS SIDE B

SEX IN DALLAS AND BILADOLL
GRAND OPENING EP

A1/GRAND OPENING//A2/THREADS //B1/THREADS KIDNAP'S PITCH BLACK LAKE MIX//B2/GRAND OPENING KONDYLOM REMIX BY GULTAR//33RPM

ALL TRACKS WRITTEN AND COMPOSED BY ADRIEN WALTER/MIA VON MATT/DAVID DUCARROS / COPYRIGHT CONTROL//B1 ADDITIONAL REMIX PRODUCTION BY KIDNAP/THORSTEN MINNING AND CORINNA VOGIC/WWW.THEKIDNAP.NET//B2 ADDITIONAL REMIX PRODUCTION BY GULTAB WHO APPEARS COURTESY OF CARELESS/ALL TRACKS RECORDED MIXED AND PRODUCED BY KIDNAP/A2 COPRODUCED BY SEX IN DALLAS AND BILADOLL//MASTERED BY ANDREAS AT SCHNITTSTELLE//DESIGN ALORENZ BERLIN//MANUFACTURED BY HANDLE WITH CARE/MADE IN GERMANY/GEMA / P AND C KITTY-YO 2005 / WORLDWIDE DISTRIBUTION BY INTERGROOVE/FAX 0049(0)69-94547555/ORDER NO KY0S100-6/THIS IS SIDE B

LITWINENKO
REISEFIEBER EP

A1/REISEFIEBER // B1/KAUBEAT // B2/OLTIMER//45RPM

ALL TRACKS WRITTEN AND PRODUCED BY LITWINENKO/TIMING MUSIC PUBLISHING/ISABELLA MUSIKVERLAG/MASTERED BY ANDREAS AT SCHNITTSTELLE/DESIGN ALORENZ BERLIN/MANUFACTURED BY HANDLE WITH CARE IN GERMANY/GEMA//P AND C KITTY-YO 2005/WORLDWIDE DISTRIBUTION BY INTERGROOVE/FAX 0049 (0)69-94547555/ORDER NO KY0S101-6/THIS IS SIDE B

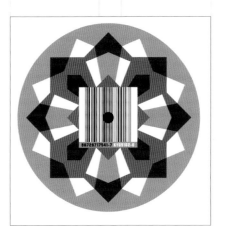

GOLD CHAINS & SUE CIE
CROWD CONTROL REMIXES

A1/CROWD CONTROL PHON.O REMIX//A2/CROWD CONTROL TOPHER LA FATA'S ALTERNATE VERSION//B1/CROWD CONTROL CB FUNK REMIX//33RPM

ALL TRACKS WRITTEN AND COMPOSED BY TOPHER LAFATA AND SUE COSTARELLE/SEASIDE CITY MUSIC//B1 ADDITIONAL REMIX PRODUCTION BY PHON.O WHO APPEARS COURTESY OF SHITKATAPULT WWW.SHITKATAPULT.COM//A2 ADDITIONAL REMIX PRODUCTION BY TOPHER LA FATA//B1 ADDITIONAL REMIX PRODUCTION BY CB FUNK WHO APPEARS COURTESY OF PUNKT MUSIC//PRODUCED BY TOPHER LA FATA/VLADISLAV DELAY/SUE COSTARILLE//RECORDED AT ZOMBIE STUDIOS SAN FRANCISCO BY UCGC/MIXED BY VLADISLAV DELAY AND TOPHER LAFATA AT RASSOUNDS BERLIN/MASTERED BY ANDREAS AT SCHNITTSTELLE / DESIGN ALORENZ BERLIN /MANUFACTURED BY HANDLE WITH CARE/MADE IN GERMANY/GEMA//UNDER EXCLUSIVE LICENSE OF KILL ROCK STARS / P KILL ROCK STARS / C KITTY-CUTS 2005//WORLDWIDE DISTRIBUTION BY INTERGROOVE/FAX 49(0)69-94 54 75 55/ORDER NO KY0S102-6//SIDE B

KITTY CUTS

Design: Angela Lorenz at
alorenz, Berlin/Wien

Taking the name of the series at face
value (in German "cut" is "Schnitt" and
"intersection" is "Schnittmenge"), Angela
Lorenz constructed the design for these
12in EP labels by appearing to cut into
the central square that holds the bar code.
Rotating, enlarging, and repeating this shape
along its diagonal forms a star shape that
resembles images created by a kaleidoscope
or the cut of a jewel. Although Lorenz isn't
working with a traditional horizontal/
vertical grid, the resulting forms are
repetitive and geometrically derived.

GRID SPECIFICATIONS

Page size (trimmed)	100 x 100mm
Top margin	To bleed
Bottom margin	To bleed
Outside margin	To bleed
Inside margin	To bleed
Number of columns	N/A
Gutter width	N/A
Extras	Grid developed from base unit—
	32mm square

I would not use the word minimal to describe my music. This is a fixed term for other music from other times. I'd rather call it economic...

Introduction »

Reciprocess + / vs.

reciprocal adj. • n. 1 in return. 2 mutual. 3 inversely correspondent; complementary.

process n. • v. 1 a course of action or procedure, esp. a series of stages in manufacture or some other operation. 2 the progress or course of something. 3 a natural or involuntary operation or series of changes. 4 (computing) operate on (data) by means of a program.

BiP-HOp in association with Fällt are pleased to present Reciprocess + /vs. A series of split CDs featuring the work(s) of two sound assemblers contributing and documenting the process of musical reciprocality between them.

This first installment features two sound assemblers contributing a collaborative work, a series of independent works, and finally, contributing a remix of each other's work(s).

Reciprocess + / vs. is co-curated by Philippe Petit (BiP-HOp) and Christopher Murphy (Fällt) and features artwork by Fällt designers Fehler.

I like the basic idea of the computer being a machine that works for you. My main applications are like organisms – living creatures. Once you've made friends with them you can rely on them and become a team.

I like precise impulsive so[unds], sine waves and white no[ise], which are both [sta]ble and clear.

I'm a bit uncontrolled and easily distracted, but this allows my compositions to be guided by the circumstances of the moment.

I have a constant impatience with my own sound, seeking to devolve and simplify it, whilst leaving an emotional content.

I would not use the word minimal to describe my music. This is a fixed term for other music from other times. I'd rather call it economic...

Reciprocess +/vs.

reciprocal adj. + n. 1 in return. 2 mutual. 3 inversely correspondent; complementary.

process n. + v. 1 a course of action or procedure, esp. a series of stages in manufacture or some other operation. 2 the progress or course of something. 3 a natural or involuntary operation or series of changes. 4 (computing) operate on (data) by means of a program.

BiP-HOp in association with Fällt are pleased to present Reciprocess +/vs. A series of split CDs featuring the work(s) of two sound assemblers and documenting the process of musical reciprocality between them.

This first installment features two sound assemblers contributing a collaborative work, a series of independent works; and finally, contributing a remix of each other's work(s).

Reciprocess +/vs. is co-curated by Philippe Petit (BiP-HOp) and Christophe Murphy (Fällt) and features artwork by Fällt designers Fehler.

GRID SPECIFICATIONS

Page size (trimmed)	120 x 120mm
Top margin	12mm
Bottom margin	12mm
Outside margin	12mm
Inside margin	12mm
Number of columns	3
Gutter width	6mm
Extras	Baseline grid, 12.7mm; 3 horizontal fields

+/VS.

Design: Fehler

This series of CDs features soundworks by two different artists. Each contributes solo tracks as well as remixing the other's work, so the brief was to create a design that didn't privilege one artist over the other. A democratic solution was achieved by creating a grid that reads in four directions: right side up for one artist, right side down for the other, with the other two axes left to hold commentary and essays.

Posters & fliers

Grids: Creative Solutions for Graphic Designers

GRID SPECIFICATIONS

Page size (trimmed)	100 x 700mm
Top margin	21mm
Bottom margin	21mm
Outside margin	21mm
Inside margin	21mm
Number of columns	38
Gutter width	37mm
Extras	Front: 10 horizontal fields
	Back: 17 horizontal fields

SUNSHINE

Design: Airside

This foldout double-sided poster was designed for DNA Films as a gift for the crew involved in making the movie *Sunshine*. The back of the poster shows the crew listed as though members of a space mission. The grid wasn't determined by content and page size alone. It was planned so that images of over 400 crew members, and all relevant information, would fit on one side of the poster without any picture or text running over the three folds.

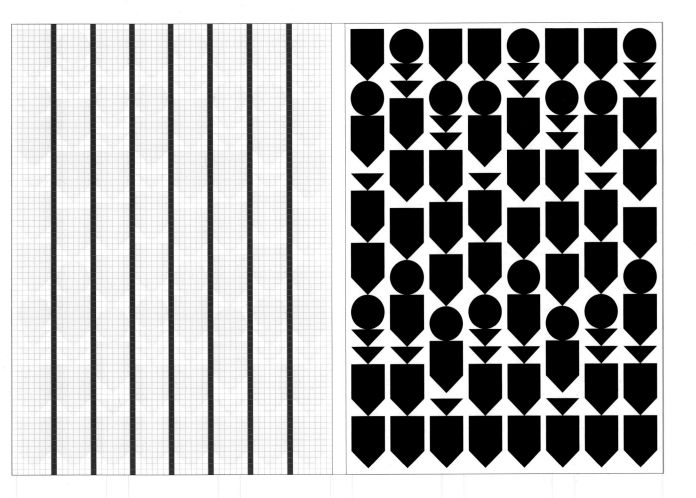

GRID SPECIFICATIONS

Page size (trimmed)	Resizable, as required
Top margin	1 base unit
Bottom margin	1 base unit
Outside margin	1 base unit
Inside margin	1 base unit
Number of columns	Flexible
Gutter width	1 base unit
Extras	Grid developed from base unit—square

FAD GRAPHIC GUIDELINE

Design: BaseDESIGN

Three basic shapes—the square, the triangle, and the circle—form
the core of the graphic system of BaseDESIGN's identity for FAD,
a Spanish, not-for-profit cultural body promoting design, architecture,
and art. The grid is determined by multiples of these forms, creating
vertical and horizontal bands across the page. These bands are then
used as columns and fields would be in a conventional grid.

Encuentros
Camper
FAD

Campana Brothers

Conferència
01.12 / 19:30h
FAD

CAMPER fad

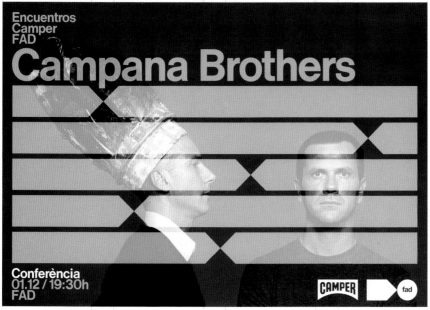

Encuentros
Camper
FAD

Campana Brothers

Conferència
01.12 / 19:30h
FAD

CAMPER fad

Grids: Creative Solutions for Graphic Designers

PERSONAL PROJECT

Design: George Adams

This is a personal project documenting a week in the life of designer George Adams. Every hour of the day is represented typographically, using categories such as "my location" and "my last conversation" to help the viewer navigate the piece. Adams was interested in how standard A paper sizes could be divided into areas that would represent units of time. When folded down to A4 (210 x 297mm [c. 8⅛ x 11⅝in]), only the first day is visible—the full week is revealed when the sheet is opened out to A1 (594 x 841mm [c. 23½ x 33in]).

GRID SPECIFICATIONS

Page size (trimmed)	A1 (594 x 841mm [c. 23½ x 33in]) folded down to A4 (210 x 297mm [c. 8⅛ x 11⅝in])
Top margin	All sheets: 10mm
Bottom margin	All sheets: 10mm
Outside margin	A1, A2, and A3: 10mm/A4: 70mm
Inside margin	All sheets: 10mm
Number of columns	A1: 4/A2: 3/A3: 2/A4: 1
Gutter width	5mm
Extras	Baseline grid, 10mm

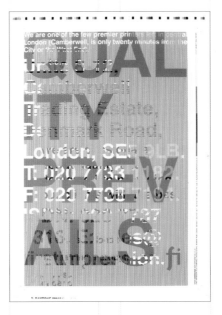

GRID SPECIFICATIONS

Page size (trimmed)	495 x 694mm
Top margin	67mm
Bottom margin	40mm
Outside margin	40mm
Inside margin	40mm
Number of columns	1
Gutter width	N/A
Extras	N/A

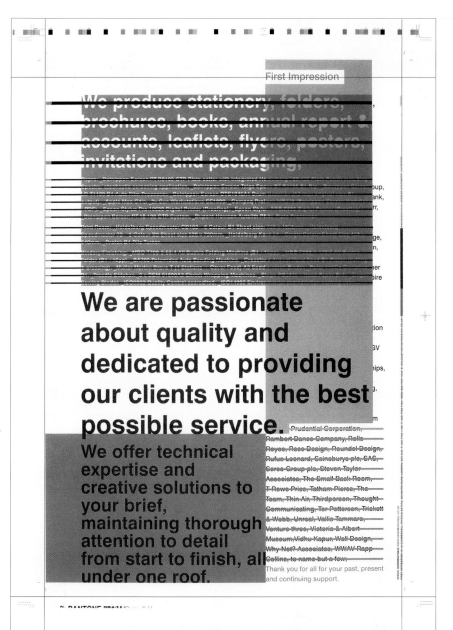

FIRST IMPRESSION

Design: Julian Harriman-Dickinson
at Harriman Steel

When Julian Harriman-Dickinson was asked to design a new business mailer for a printing company, he decided to turn the brief into a challenge to create the most difficult print job the printers had ever worked on. These five posters use overprinting to showcase the high quality of registration and print. From the first print run of 5,000, 1,000 were sent out, and the remaining 4,000 were overprinted with more information; 1,000 of these were sent out, and so on, until all the mailers had been distributed. In this way, any underlying structure was gradually revealed.

Luke Wood is the Head of Design at the University of Canterbury and a practising designer. He designed and exhibited a typeface replicating the script of Colin McCahon's word paintings, and recently held a residency at Hatch Show Prints in Nashville.

Hamish Thompson is the author and designer of Paste-up: A Century of New Zealand Poster Art. Trained at the Basel School of Design in Switzerland, he has taught, written about and practised design for over 20 years.

Catherine Griffiths is an innovative typographer who designed the BEST Design Award-winning Wellington Writers Walk and gave a new meaning to concrete poetry. Design from her Wellington studio, Epitome, spans print and architecture.

OLD SCHOOL

NEW SCHOOL

TRUETYPE SCHOOL

3 DESIGNERS SPEAK

Hamish Thompson 'Poster Design'
Mon 15 Aug 12-1pm
St David 1

Catherine, Hamish & Luke Tues 16
Open Lecture Aug 6.30pm
Archway 3

Catherine & Luke 'Design & Typography'
seminar Wed 17 Aug 1-2pm
Design Studies CApSc 1.05

Brought to you by:

New Zealand Print Culture Area of Research Strength

DINZ (Designers Institute of New Zealand)

Design Studies | Te Toki a Rata

UNIVERSITY OTAGO

GRID SPECIFICATIONS

Page size (trimmed)	400 x 600mm
Top margin	N/A
Bottom margin	N/A
Outside margin	N/A
Inside margin	50mm
Number of columns	8
Gutter width	N/A
Extras	Grid developed from base unit—rectangle with ratio of 2:3; baseline grid, 22pt; 8 horizontal fields

OLD SCHOOL, NEW SCHOOL, TRUETYPE SCHOOL
Design: Lightship Visual

This poster was designed for a series of graphic design lectures at the University of Otago, New Zealand. The surface area of the poster is divided to form eight vertical and eight horizontal fields. The gray background provides a neutral ground for colored rectangular panels that correspond with this underlying system of organization and draw attention to the poster's structure. Designer Stuart Medley's decision to foreground the grid as an organizing principle was informed by the panel of speakers, which included designers taught by Emil Ruder and Wolfgang Weingart.

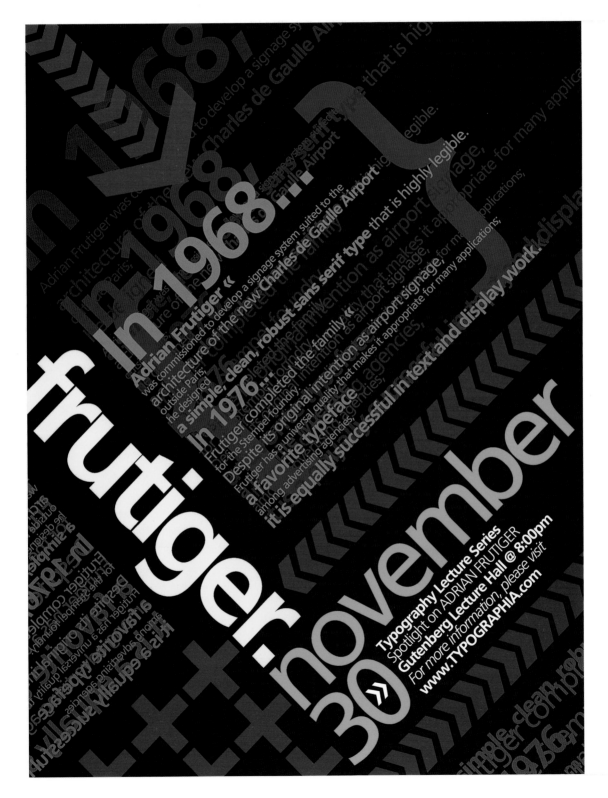

In 1968...
Adrian Frutiger was commissioned to develop a signage system suited to the architecture of the new Charles de Gaulle Airport outside Paris;

In 1976...
Frutiger completed the family for the Stempel foundry;

Adrian Frutiger «

a simple, clean, robust sans serif type that is highly legible.

Despite its original intention as airport signage, Frutiger has a universal quality that makes it appropriate for many applications;

a favorite typeface among advertising agencies;

it is equally successful in text and display work.

frutiger.

november 30

Typography Lecture Series
Spotlight on ADRIAN FRUTIGER
Gutenberg Lecture Hall @ 8:00pm
For more information, please visit
www.TYPOGRAPHIA.com

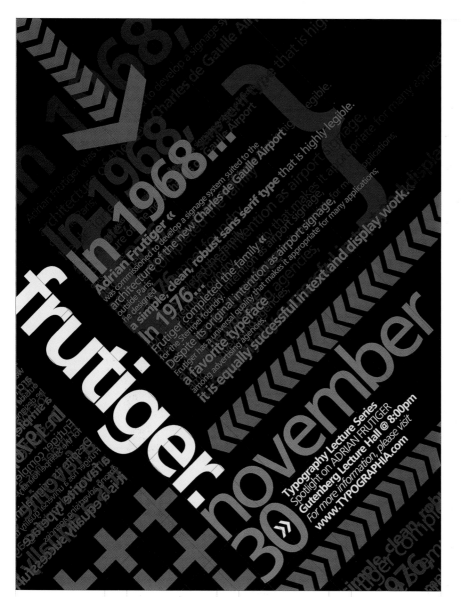

GRID SPECIFICATIONS

Page size (trimmed)	457.2 x 609.6mm
Top margin	To bleed
Bottom margin	To bleed
Outside margin	To bleed
Inside margin	To bleed
Number of columns	11
Column gutter	N/A
Extras	rotated grid;
	8 horizontal fields

FRUTIGER POSTER

Design: Reggie Hidalgo at
The Art Institute of California

This poster promotes a lecture series
on typography, in particular, the work of
Adrian Frutiger. It uses a series of angled
alignments. The poster is divided into
11 columns and eight horizontal fields.
Although this isn't a conventional grid,
composed of equal columns or fields
and gutters, it is reminiscent of the
organizational approach followed by
exponents of the Swiss school in the design
of posters. Using these methods, art director
Maggie Rossoni and designer Reggie
Hidalgo have created a dynamic piece of
design information that is easy to navigate.

tHe BaBySHAMBLES SESSiONS 1, 2 & 3

available for download from : http: / www.babyshambles.net

....at the end of his tether, Barât quit the session halfway through. Doherty, true to form, made the abandoned demos available for free on the internet, calling them The Babyshambles Sessions.

the
BABYSHAMBLES SESSiONS
1, 2 & 3

available for download from : http: www.babyshambles.net
...at the end of his tether, Barât quit the session halfway through. Doherty, true to form, made the abandoned demos available for free on the internet, calling them The Babyshambles Sessions.

GRID SPECIFICATIONS

Page size (trimmed)	580 x 990mm
Top margin	170mm
Bottom margin	20mm
Outside margin	30mm
Inside margin	40mm
Number of columns	26
Gutter width	N/A
Extras	40 horizontal rows

BABYSHAMBLES SESSIONS

Design: Peter Crnokrak at ±

The Babyshambles Sessions are a series of studio sessions by The Libertines recorded a few months before their breakup and made available as free downloads by Pete Doherty. This promotional poster prototype features a grid of 3,050 1 x 1cm squares—each hand-colored using Pantone Tria markers on Lambda Duraflex—that make up an image of Doherty's face. Designer Peter Crnokrak wanted the hand-colored squares to communicate the contrast between the digital medium of the sessions and the lo-fi acoustic content of the music.

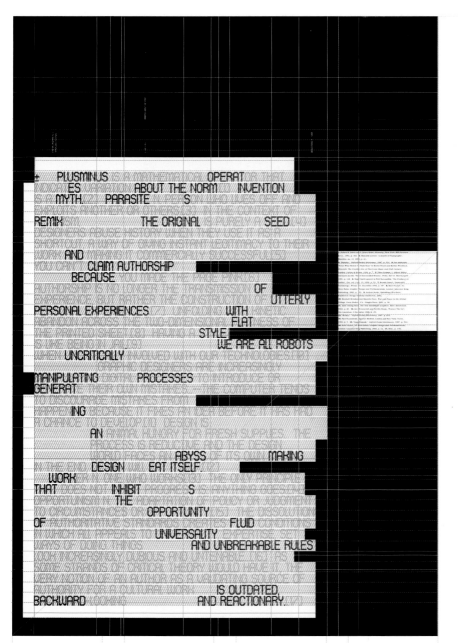

GRID SPECIFICATIONS

Page size (trimmed)	840 x 1,170mm
Top margin	193mm
Bottom margin	41mm
Outside margin	154mm
Inside margin	49mm
Number of columns	4
Gutter width	N/A
Extras	8 horizontal fields, 6 lines per field

WORKER/PARASITE MANIFESTO

Design: Peter Crnokrak at ±

The ± worker/parasite manifesto uses appropriated statements and graphics "remixed" by designer Peter Crnokrak. The original quotes all relate in some form to notions of originality, authorship, and rules (including the use of the grid) in graphic design. These are printed in light-gray horizontal lines that can only be read from a certain distance, while the ± manifesto text is highlighted in black, thereby making clear what is a paradox for Crnokrak.

love will tear us apart again.

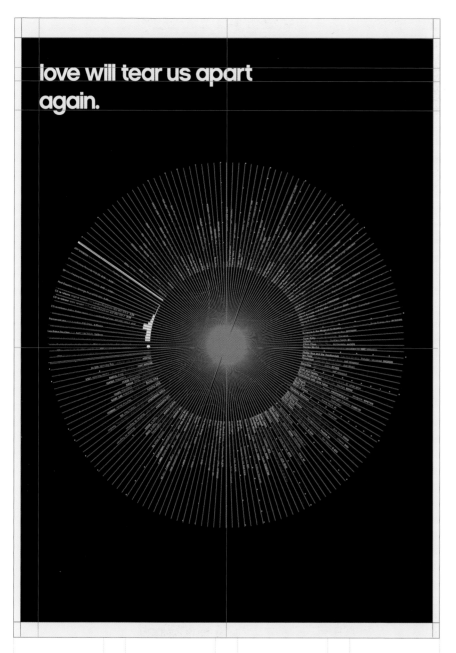

love will tear us apart again.

GRID SPECIFICATIONS

Page size (trimmed)	594 x 841mm
Top margin	27.5mm
Bottom margin	9.7mm
Outside margin	9.7mm
Inside margin	9.7mm
Number of columns	N/A
Gutter width	N/A
Extras	N/A

LOVE WILL TEAR US APART AGAIN
Design: Peter Crnokrak at ±

This poster uses the principles of information design to compare over 85 cover versions of Joy Division's "Love Will Tear Us Apart Again." Each version is mapped to show how long after the original it was recorded, along with the recording artist, release name and date, and label. The design uses the visually seductive device of lines radiating from a circle to structure the information. The print on off-white, heavy-weight art paper is a nod to the original graphic material produced for Joy Division by designer Peter Saville.

GRID SPECIFICATIONS

Page size (trimmed)	1,200 x 1,700mm
Top margin	28mm
Bottom margin	28mm
Outside margin	28mm
Inside margin	28mm
Number of columns	6
Gutter width	16mm
Extras	Baseline grid, 48pt

I LOVE TÁVORA

Design: Lizá Ramalho, Artur Rebelo, and Liliana Pinto at R2 design

This poster promotes a series of events that were tributes to modernist Portuguese architect Fernando Távora. Designers Lizá Ramalho and Artur Rebelo wanted the poster to evoke the ideological and philosophical principles that characterize Távora's work. The text is laid out using a six-column grid, but most of the poster is filled with a typographic composition suggestive of an urban plan, within which a heart can be seen.

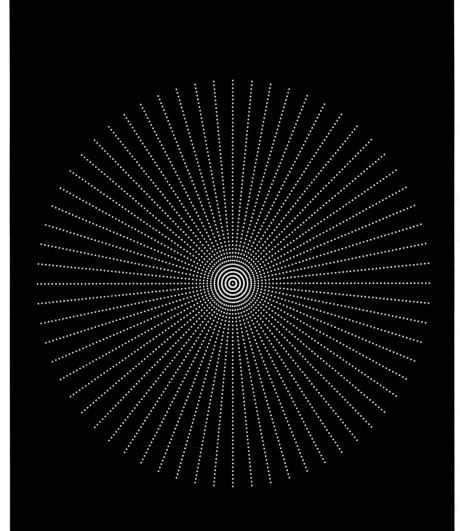

ON/OFF

A Sound Seminar Thursday 15th December 6pm RCafé

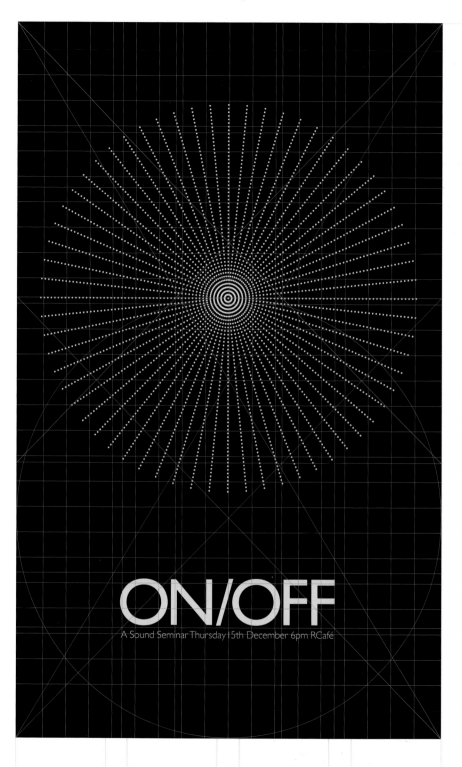

A Sound Seminar Thursday 15th December 6pm RCafé

ON/OFF

GRID SPECIFICATIONS

Page size (trimmed)	512 x 832mm
Top margin	32mm
Bottom margin	32mm
Outside margin	32mm
Inside margin	32mm
Number of columns	16
Gutter width	N/A
Extras	Baseline grid, 3.2mm; 28 fields

ON/OFF

Design: Richard Sarson

This poster advertised a series of seminars
on sound that were held at the Royal
College of Art, London, where Richard
Sarson was a student. Inspired by Josef
Müller-Brockmann and Jan Tschichold,
Sarson used abstract shapes to explore
visual representations of rhythm and
sound, and looked to geometry to develop
his grid by taking the golden section as his
starting point.

Grids: Creative Solutions for Graphic Designers

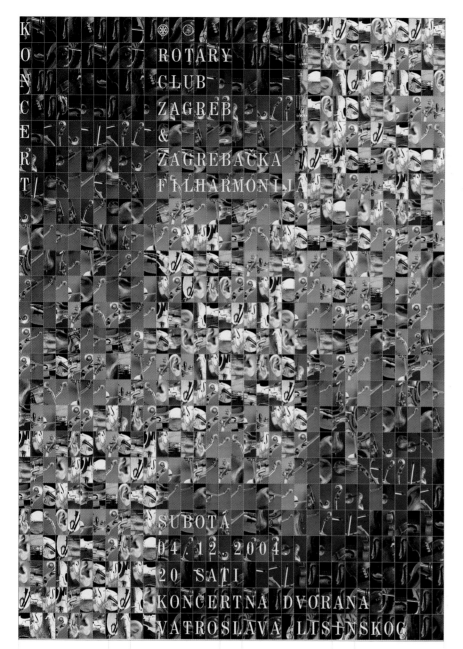

GRID SPECIFICATIONS

Page size (trimmed)	700 x 1,000mm
Top margin	To bleed
Bottom margin	To bleed
Outside margin	To bleed
Inside margin	To bleed
Number of columns	34
Gutter width	N/A
Extras	Grid developed from base unit— portrait rectangle

ROTARY CLUB PHILHARMONIC CONCERT

Design: Boris Ljubicic at Studio International

Designer Boris Ljubicic's creative inspiration for this concert poster was the three-tonal scale of the music. The poster is divided into a grid of narrow columns and fields, each filled with an image to form a mosaic of photographs—a visual representation of the rich orchestral music to be played at the concert. Ljubicic describes the process of importing these images into the grid as similar to composing virtual music.

GRID SPECIFICATIONS

Page size (trimmed)	1,400 x 1,000mm
Top margin	To bleed
Bottom margin	To bleed
Outside margin	To bleed
Inside margin	To bleed
Number of columns	16; 8 per image
Gutter width	N/A
Extras	Grid is broken along vertical columns to intersperse two separate images

3-D POSTERS

Design: Boris Ljubicic at Studio International

Boris Ljubicic's intention in designing these posters for the Croatian National Tourist Board was to provide a contrast to the conventional photographic poster aimed at vacationers. These posters are three dimensional, with the folds forming the grid. Photographs of traditional tourist sites are juxtaposed with images of tourists themselves in order to encourage viewer curiosity and participation. When viewed from different angles, the posters show an alternative image.

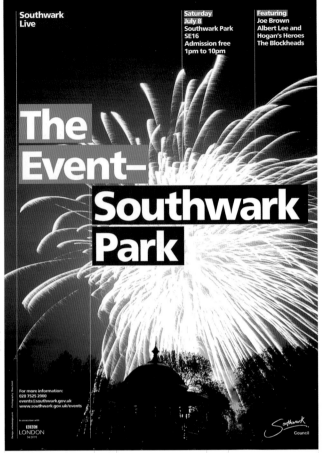

SOUTHWARK LIVE

Design: Tim Sawford at Wire

Southwark Live is one of London's largest events programs.
Wire's brief was to create a functional and flexible visual identity to
convey the vibrancy and diversity of the activities on offer. Designer
Tim Sawford used abstract forms, inspired by the flags often seen
at local events, within a multicolumn and multifield system. Colored
text boxes help to make informational hierarchy clear even against
the more complex photographic images.

GRID SPECIFICATIONS

Page size (trimmed)	297 x 420mm
Top margin	10mm
Bottom margin	13.5mm
Outside margin	12mm
Inside margin	8.5mm
Number of columns	16
Gutter width	4mm
Extras	Baseline grid, 0.5mm

MyHome SIEBEN
SEVEN EXPERIMENTE
EXPERIMENTS FÜR EIN NEUES
FOR
CONTEMPORARY
LIVING Interventions WOHNEN Interventionen
by: von:

Jurgen Bey, Ronan & Erwan Bouroullec, Fernando & Humberto Campana, Hella Jongerius, Greg Lynn, Jürgen Mayer H., Jerszy Seymour

EINE AUSSTELLUNG
AN EXHIBITION
AT THE IM
VITRA DESIGN MUSEUM
14. JUNI—
16. SEPTEMBER
2007

Opening hours			Öffnungszeiten		
Monday–Sunday	10 am–6 pm		Montag–Sonntag	10–18 Uhr	
Wednesday	10 am–8 pm		Mittwoch	10–20 Uhr	
Guided tours			Führungen		
Saturday and Sunday	11 am		Samstag und Sonntag	11 Uhr	

Vitra Design Museum
Charles-Eames-Strasse. 1 / D-79576 Weil am Rhein
info-weil@design-museum.de / www.design-museum.de
phone +49 (0)7621 / 702 3200
fax +49 (0)7621 / 702 3590

Vitra Design Museum

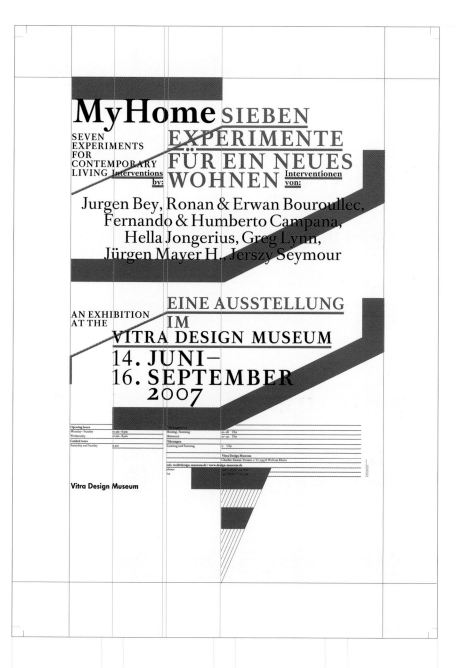

Page size (trimmed)	895 x 1,280mm
Top margin	85mm
Bottom margin	100mm
Outside margin	100mm
Inside margin	100mm
Number of columns	4
Gutter width	N/A
Extras	N/A

MY HOME

Design: Ludovic Balland

This poster for the exhibition Seven Experiments for Contemporary Living, held at the Vitra Design Museum, is obviously very much about structure, although a traditional grid has been employed only partially. Designer Ludovic Balland used two-dimensional abstract forms to denote three-dimensional spaces, creating two trapezium-shaped "rooms" to be filled with typographic information.

Index